Enjoy Laughing at Life

with me!

[signature]

Laughing at Life

Situational humor
for writers, speakers,
and all who laugh

Lyle Manery

Laughing Brings Us Closer Together

Lyalta Publishing
1403 - 2nd St. S.W.
Calgary, Alberta T2R 0W7
Telephone: (403) 233-2558
Fax: (403) 266-7078
Orders: 1-888-322-2558

Cover Design: Jon Paine
Illustrations: Diana Fox
Editor: John King

National Library of Canada Cataloguing in Publication Data

Manery, Lyle, 1935–
Laughing at life:
Situational humor for writers,
speakers, and all who laugh
ISBN 0-9699101-8-5

1. Canadian wit and humor (English) I. Title.
PN6147.M35 2001   C818'.5402   C2001-901371-X

A Laugh a Day

We need to laugh more! Actually we need to learn to laugh again. Don't you agree people are forgetting their sense of humor these days? People are getting so serious they can't even laugh at themselves. If we can but laugh at the situation we find ourselves in, often caused by our own actions, we will live longer. Not only will we live longer, but we'll be happier too. Obviously, those around us will enjoy us more if we are *happy*.

An article published by Maritime Life (in its "Lifetime" series) states that: "Research clearly indicates that laughter is good medicine. Humor makes hospital patients happy. And happy patients usually promote their own recovery by working harder at it. A good laugh is more than curative medicine. It is also preventative medicine."

As we get older, we laugh less. Loretta LaRoche of "The Humor Potential" says:

Do you know that when you're age four you laugh four hundred times a day? By the time you are an adult, you're lucky if you are cranking out fifteen a day, and they sound like this— "ahuhhuha, ahuhhuha." *As preventative medicine you should be laughing as often as possible.*

Will Rogers advised us: "We are here for a spell; get all the laughs you can!"

Michael P. McKinley, CSP, CPAE, says: "Every day I look at things and try to find some stuff to laugh at. I found this sign in a store. It says 'all children running loose and unattended will be towed and stored at owners' expense.'" Another sign that Michael enjoys was found posted on a farmer's fence: "Warning. Don't cross this field unless you can do it in 9.9 seconds. The bull can do it in 10 seconds."

1

Laughter increases your red blood cell count. The tears that come from laughter are of a different chemical composition than those that come from crying. Laughing is one of the healthiest things you can do to reduce stress—second only to making love to your spouse. Notice I said *spouse*. Doctors claim that adulterous affairs create feelings of anxiety and guilt that manifest themselves in ill health. Furthermore, you could get shot. So if you really want to be healthy, laugh when you make love to your spouse. Come to think of it, that could get you shot too!

A good laugh can reverse all the body's stress responses by the release of endorphins. The next time you get stuck in traffic, turn off the distressing news on the radio and turn on a tape of your favorite comedian. You'll be the only one in your lane laughing. You may be the only one with normal blood pressure. When you say, "My heart is heavy with sadness," your heart is literally loaded with sad chemicals. When you say, "I'm bursting with joy," your skin secrets high levels of antidepressants. These compounds are not merely antidepressants but they are also powerful modulators that can alter the immune system.

Stress and negative feelings play a large part in the impairment of an immune system. Conversely, positive laughter-induced emotions actually boost the body's immune functions. Laughter stimulates your internal organs and helps reduce blood pressure. It promotes relaxation. Laughter can diffuse potentially explosive situations. A healthy belly laugh will cause an improvement in respiration, which in turn promotes healthy increases in the heart rate and blood circulation.

Dr. William Fry of the Stanford Medical School likens laughter to "inner jogging." One therapist suggests that laughing one hundred times a day is the cardiovascular equivalent of ten minutes of rowing.

William James, a renowned American psychologist, wrote, "We don't laugh because we're happy—we're happy because we laugh."

According to Gene Perret, author of *Comedy Writing Step by Step*, "There are few good judges of comedy and we don't agree."

We all tend to think we are experts when it comes to what is humorous. Joseph Sorban says, "The trouble with experts is that, because they know more than anyone else, they forgot how much they don't know."

Of course, we all know that old saw, "Experts tend to know more and more about less and less until eventually they know all there is to know about nothing."

Truer words have never been spoken than the following: "An expert is a person with a briefcase, ten miles from home." Obviously, everyone is an expert when it comes to what is personally enjoyable. However, many of us have an opinion of what others should like or dislike. In this book, we have attempted to provide humorous stories and anecdotes that will stimulate emotional well-being. We have attempted to provide examples that make a point. Humor can be found in satire, sarcasm, truth, exaggeration, conundrum, oxymoron, tension, distortion, shocking content, and authority figures.

Be assured, it is not our intent to offend anyone. On the other hand, everyone's sense of humor is different, and everyone's opinion of what is humorous is highly individualistic. It would be improbable to relate a broad variety of situational stories that appeal to everyone A few of the stories included here were rejected by some people as not so funny. However, I have told every one of them to others who did find them humorous. Thank you!

Remember the old adage, "You cannot please all of the people all of the time." If you are not amused by some of the stories that I have included, turn to the person on your left. If she is laughing, turn to the person on your right. If he is laughing—well...! It could be you. Maybe you should read it again.

To eliminate all risqué stories would result in a rather mundane presentation. It is important to keep in mind that there is no intent in these pages to belittle or demean any race, creed, color, or whatever. We are attempting to illustrate that the situation is humorous. We are laughing *with* people rather than *at* them.

My wife Betty and my good friend Allan Johnson have acted as censors, at my request, to screen stories, anecdotes, and comments that they deemed inappropriate. In fairness to them, I confess that some of the material in these pages did not meet their strict standards. Some of it slipped in without them seeing it, because I learned to type a little. As the author of this book, I had final say. *I am responsible!*

Enjoy it as it was intended and laugh your way to good health. Many people have contributed material that has been included in this book. To acknowledge them all would take too much space. I have collected these jokes and anecdotes over the past forty years. Wherever possible, I have given credit to the person from whom I first heard it.

I cannot be sure about originality. However, I have tried to avoid jokes published on the Internet or in other publications. Nevertheless, some published material has been included for special reasons, which hopefully will be obvious. In my experience, most humorous material has been revamped from other stories and retold to fit the situation. Thus, the origin of some stories may not be clear, and no one has a special claim on the version being presented.

True humor is a partnership.
It's equal parts humorist and audience!

North Carolina basketball coach Joseph T. Valvano says, "So here is my philosophy of getting the job done. A pinch of laughter each day is important. I think you should laugh every day."

People all over the world are in insane asylums or institutions because they take themselves too seriously. You have to learn to laugh with others and at yourself. If, when you get older, you look in the mirror and you can't laugh—boy, you've got problems.

Joel Goodman says, "Humor prevents a hardening of the attitudes."

Woody Allen says, "Most of the time, I don't have much fun. The rest of the time I don't have any at all."

Abe Lincoln said, "People are about as happy as they will allow themselves to be. Therefore, a pessimist is a person who, when confronted with two unpleasant alternatives, selects them both."

Disraeli claimed that "Action may not always bring happiness, but there is no happiness without action."

Richard Bach, author of *Illusions,* said, "In order to live free and happily, you must sacrifice boredom. It's always not an easy sacrifice."

Samuel Almon wrote, "We do not grow old by simply living a number of years. We grow old when we lose our fun, our zest for life; for that wrinkles the soul."

One of my favorite authors is a Greek philosopher named Anonymous. Anonymous said, "To laugh is to risk appearing the fool. To weep is to risk appearing sentimental. To reach out to another is to risk involvement, and to expose your feelings is to risk exposing your true self."

Aristotle observed, "There is a foolish corner of the brain of the wisest man."

Abraham Maslowe said, "To laugh at what you hold sacred and still hold it sacred, is the highest form of humor."

I'm trying to arrange my life
so that I don't even have to be present.

Humor is everywhere around you, if you look for it.

Love to laugh! Laugh to love! Hearing other people laugh is enjoyable. It is even more fun for me when I can be the cause of some hilarity. A comedian I am not, although I have been called worse. Stand-up comedy has never been something that I could see myself doing. Spreading anecdotal humor among my friends, telling jokes on the golf course, or entertaining informally at a party is something I have always done.

Hardly a day goes by in which I do not use humor to brighten the lives of those around me. It's not a duty. I don't feel obligated. I just enjoy doing it, and, generally, people seem to enjoy it, which, of course, encourages me to continue. I love to hear people laugh.

Now don't get me wrong. I usually have time to listen to someone else telling a joke, even if I have heard it before. If I know the punch line, I listen to the technique or style. Sometimes the storyteller surprises me with a different punch line.

Occasionally, the way the story is told is more humorous than the story itself. One of my golfing buddies relates a funny incident in such a delightful way that I encourage him to tell it every chance I get. A new guy in the foursome always gets to hear it. My attitude is, if you don't enjoy hearing it again, go wash your ball or repair some divots. I listen to see and to hear the reaction of our guest.

Emery has several regular jokes that he likes to tell. Often he comes up with new ones. He is a partner in a restaurant, and obviously he hears a large variety of humor. In relating any of Emery's stories here, I am limited to the written word. The best part of all of his stories is the way he does it. To attempt to capture his expressions and gestures in writing would take more space than the anecdote. So, let me give you my version of one of my favorites—a golf classic:

One day, the foursome was discussing how they got their wives to agree to a Saturday morning golf game. Joe, the oldest of the foursome, said, "Well I gave my wife a really nice bouquet of flowers."

Larry, the quietest of the group, said, "Well, for the past week, I did chores around the house: dishes, dusting, and vacuuming."

George, the tallest and most talkative of the group, stated, "It was no problem, I just gave her my credit card and told her to go shopping."

Everyone turned to Emery for his explanation. "Well, it's a lot easier than you think. When I woke up at 6:30, I just reached over to my wife, shook her gently and asked, 'Dear what do you say, intercourse or the golf course?' She opened one eye and said, "Don't forget your jacket."

It's even funnier when Emery tells it. Emery is often a source of humorous incidents on the golf course. He is relatively quiet, so, when he says something or does something, we take notice.

On one occasion, our fourth couldn't make it, so we were about to go out as a threesome. A young lady, a gorgeous young lady, who often worked in the pro shop, asked if she could join us. We agreed without hesitation. Anne informed us that she would appreciate any tips and help we could offer. She mentioned that she had just recently taken to the game of golf.

On the second hole, a par three over water, Anne made a super drive and landed on the green. Her first putt brought her ball to within three feet of the pin. As she looked the putt over, she stated that she would be *very* appreciative toward anyone of us who could help her make this putt. In her golfing to date, she had never made a par. This was a great opportunity. I studied the line and advised her to shoot about one inch to the right of the hole.

Les looked it over and said, "No, she should aim at the left side of the hole."

The next thing I saw was Emery on his hands and knees looking closely at the matter. After a poignant pause, Emery looked at Anne and said, "Close enough, it's a gimme."

I've been in one bunker so often I get my mail there!

The following week, at our regular time, Anne was working in the pro shop. My three golf buddies lined up ahead of me to pay their fees.

They got the senior's rate. When I went to sign my credit card, I noticed that she charged me full price. I asked her if I didn't warrant a senior's discount.

She looked at me and asked, "Do you qualify?"

"Sure," I replied. "I'm older than any of those guys."

She smiled at me, "Well you don't look it."

All right! I signed the credit charge at full price.

What do you mean, any lovely young lady can wow any old man?

Another one of my golfing buddies loves to tell about the following incident. It cracks him up whenever he tells it. Sometimes we laugh too. His laugh is infectious.

As he tells it, it seems that two of his acquaintances were golfing at Mountainside, Fairmont, in British Columbia. I won't mention their names to protect the guilty. Anyway, our two stars were playing as a twosome. On the tenth hole, they decided to spice up the game. They agreed to a friendly wager for the back nine. They would play skins for $100. For those who do not know the term "skins," it means simply that each hole would be worth $100 to the winner. A tie means no money would change hands. In other words, you have to win to win.

Both golfers had reasonable drives off the tee. Both of them fired second shots to the left, somewhat below the elevated green.

From there, you can just see the top of the flagpole. On their third strokes, both made good shots, right at the pin. When they got to the top of the green, they discovered that one ball was on the lip of the hole. The other ball was in the hole. They were both playing a Titleist Number 1.

"Now what?" queried golfer number one?

"I don't know," answered number two. "Let's ask the pro."

When they arrived back at the hole with Lorne Rowe, the golf pro, they explained their dilemma.

After looking it over, Lorne stated, "Well gentlemen, I think I can solve your little problem. Which one of you was shooting the white ball and which one was using the orange ball?"

You can see a pro needs lots of people skills.

Sometimes, we are guilty of making foolish or careless assumptions that may be embarrassing, but, with luck, there could be some humor in the situation. For instance:

On one occasion I was a guest of Don, Bronko, and Jim, three other golfing friends, at their home club. We were on the first tee. Another club member, known to be a stickler for the rules (just like my editor) approached the tee just as Bronko was addressing his ball, three feet in front of the markers.

In a somewhat testy voice, the rules stickler commented, "My good man, don't you know the rules of golf? You're supposed to tee off behind those markers.

Bronko looked up and in an even voice replied: "First of all, I am not your good man. Second, I do understand the rules of golf. Third, this happens to be my second shot."

Several years ago, when I was active in Jaycees (Junior Chamber of Commerce), I spent a pleasant evening in a small town in northern Alberta—High Level. That evening, I learned a few valuable lessons. I was the after-dinner speaker.

It seemed as though the whole town turned out—not just the local Jaycees. The mayor and several town councilors were introduced. The local MLA was present. The town manager and his staff were in the audience. Unbeknownst to me, there was also a newspaper reporter present.

During my talk, I referred to one of our treasured Jaycee themes: "Young men and women can change the world." As an aside, I mentioned that one young man did, in fact, change the world. Hitler and his Third Reich put things in motion that may never be repaired, and Adolf Hitler will never be forgotten. The next day, newspaper headlines blared "Jaycee President Advocates Young Men Should Be More Like Hitler." I did not! However, that report followed me throughout the province. Obviously, I should have been more careful about my commentary.

Robert Frost wrote:
"Forgive me my nonsense as I also forgive the
nonsense of those who think they talk sense."

Later in the evening, a large group of young men joined me in my room to drink my scotch. Soon a joke-telling contest was instigated. This contest was a little different than you might expect. The object was to see if you could get through a joke without someone else telling the punch line. Most of us failed most of the time. This event made me understand a point. *In any audience, you may be sure that someone has heard your story before, unless it's very original.*

Several of the attempted jokes were ethnic in substance. We were a tight knit-group, so there was no chance of anyone being offended. Finally, after an hour or two, someone said, "Karl wants to tell one."

Karl was a large Ukrainian farm boy. He was about 6 foot 3 inches and weighed at least 250 pounds, with big muscles. Karl was very shy, and he had been quiet all evening. So now everyone paid attention as Karl stood to make his presentation. Karl spoke with a stutter:

"Wh-what, what's bla-black and-and bl-blue all over and li-lies wr-writhing in pain in a dit-ditch?"

No one knew the punch line. "What Karl?"

"Th-the ne-next SOB wh-who te-tells a Ukrainian joke."

There was an explosion of laughter, and Karl won our little contest.

Don't go around saying the world owes you a living. The world owes you nothing. It was here first!

Several years later, at another gathering of Jaycees, Karl again stood to tell a story. By now, Karl had gained some confidence as a speaker. Jaycees take pride in helping each other become more adept at speaking in front of an audience, developing young people for leadership. Karl was a good student, but he still had a tendency to stutter a little bit.

Karl related a story about three sales people who had been recruited to sell Bibles. The first one was a young man with lots of noticeable talent. The second one was a young lady who exuded poise and charm. The organizers had great hopes for both of them. The third applicant was a shy young man who spoke with a stutter. There did not appear to be much hope of his succeeding. However, they decided to let him try.

Later that day, the three new sales people returned to the office to report on the day's activities.

The first reported that he had sold only one new Bible, "Everyone already owns at least one Bible."

The young lady reported that she had sold seven Bibles. "Some Bibles were worn out and needed to be replaced."

The shy young man reported that he had sold two dozen Bibles. Everyone was amazed. How could this shy young man with a stutter sell so many Bibles. "Well, I-I-I just a-asked them if-if th-th-they wou-would like to-to bu-buy one-one or-or sh-should I-I re-read it-it to-to th-them?"

> ### Writers, speakers, and communicators are good liars. The worst consequence of that is that they can lie to themselves and actually believe it.

When I was at Purdue University, we had a class of around thirty people from across the United States and Canada. Most of us were on campus for three months. We stayed in one wing of a motel, and we got to know each other quite well.

Whenever someone started to tell a story, someone in our group would shout out a number. Example: "32." Everyone would laugh—except the guest speakers who were not in on our humor. It was even more perplexing for some speakers, when right in the middle of the talk someone would call out a number. The number, perhaps "15," would be a joke or anecdote that was appropriate to the speaker's point. The only problem was that the speaker, not being in on it, could not understand why we laughed—seemingly at his serious statement.

☙☙☙

Writing about the above class situation reminded me of another occasion when I was on a two-week branch manager's course conducted by the Life Insurance Marketing and Research Association. Fifty managers from nearly all parts of the United States, and three from Canada, were in attendance. At the first meeting, everyone was required to stand up and tell something about themselves, their company, and their experience to date. Approximately forty classmates had spoken before the chap next to me spoke. He told us about himself and his company, and then he went on and on about the great state of Texas. To hear him talk, you would think that the only state in the nation that mattered was Texas.

Finally, it was my turn. To this point, I had heard a variety of accents. I love those parochial accents, and I knew I would be mimicking them very soon. I can't help it. But, as I stood, something made me affect an accent that no one else had—French-Canadian.

So I said, "Eh cowboy, I am from Canada, and we got enough snow there to fill the whole 'f-en' state of Texas. Everybody roared with laughter except my friend to my left. He never sat by me again during the two-week session. Oh well!

Having affected an accent of my own, I continued to use it with no exceptions. This caused many of my associates to greet me in French. Now, I am not fluent in that language, but I was better at it than any of my fellow students. You know how it is—the last one talking wins.

On one occasion, several of my associates and I went into a nearby lounge for some refreshments. I continued to use my special accent. Surprisingly, a young lady sitting at a table near us leaned over and spoke to me in French. I answered her confidently, and she fired a comment back at me without a moment's hesitation. After two or three more exchanges, I knew I was in trouble. She was too glib, and the French language just rolled off her tongue with ease. In fact, I realized she was not speaking simple high school French.

Dropping my affected accent, I asked in English where she was from.

"Paris, France," she answered with a broad smile.

My new friends from the United States chuckled with glee. I had just been exposed as a linguistic fraud.

Now if you want to tell me a joke, please avoid one type of joke if you possibly can—corny jokes. Why not corny jokes? Because I always remember them, and I cannot resist telling them to other people. Everybody groans at these "groaners," but I seem to be predisposed to tell them anyway. The only way I can resist relating groaners is if you don't tell me one.

For example: Gene Perret, in his book *Comedy Writing Step by Step,* asks the question, "Can you tell me how long cows should be milked?"

Some people answer, "Five or ten minutes."

A farm boy like me, who has milked a large number of cows, would answer, "Until she is empty."

The comic reply is "The same as short cows."

People laugh or groan because they don't expect that answer. A different meaning has been found for the question. This illustrates a couple of points. *Using an unexpected punch line can create humor.* If you can take an old joke, tell it in a *slightly different way*, and provide an all-new ending, the result can be delightful for the audience—especially those who were expecting something else. *Since the above example is a bit corny, I will never be able to resist retelling it.*

More corn:

When I was a teenager and was in our church choir, we enjoyed being involved with a little play on words. Everyone in the choir spoke German—some since birth. Naturally, when we greeted, someone would ask, "Wie geht's?" The full expressions is: "Wie geht es ihnen?" It means simply "How are you?" Translating literally, however—"How goes it with you?" Or "How do you go?"

The answer in German might be: "Auf zwei Beine." That is: "On two legs."

Another one: "Was ist los?" meaning, "What is wrong?" Translating literally into English, it would be, "What is loose?" The answer could be, "Alles was nicht fest ist." That is, "Everything that is not fastened."

It was innocent fun, and you could say it in church. One time, in the church basement, I asked a five-year-old boy, "Kannst du Deutsch sprechen? ("Can you speak German?") To the delight of all those listening, he replied, "Ja, besser als du." ("Yes, better than you.")

So much for the language lesson.

Karl Marx, as you know, authored *Das Kapital*. One day his mother said, "Karl, maybe things would be better if you spent more time making capital rather than just writing about it."

Using humor during a seminar or in a keynote talk can add a very valuable dimension to your program:

- First of all, a clever joke can get the attention of everyone in your audience.
- Second, an appropriate anecdote can give emphasis to a point you want to make.
- Third, a little humor can break up the monotony of the more technical aspects of your talk.
- Fourth, people always remember the funny content long after they have forgotten your serious content.

Telling jokes during your program or talk, which are appropriate and effective, can be a bit tricky. They can backfire, and often they do. I told two jokes in Wetaskiwin, Alberta, and they both bombed. The same two jokes in Taber, Alberta, a few nights earlier, got howls of laughter. You may respond, "Well they are different audiences; therefore, you should not expect the same success with both groups." That's true, but they did have a common denominator. Both groups were members and guests of the Junior Chamber of Commerce.

Your advice might be "Don't tell those jokes in Wetaskiwin ever again," and I never have. In fact, I have never given a talk there since. That'll teach 'em. Actually, I have never been invited back. In Taber, however, they think I am a humorist.

Chaos is the law of nature.
Order is a dream of mankind!

You may be curious as to the jokes I told that received such variable reaction in these two cities. So I will tell you.

Early in both talks, I stated that I had stopped off on the way to the meeting at a nearby Indian reservation and presented my talk to an assembly arranged by the Chief in an outside arena. My stated motive was to practice my material before a live audience.

Throughout my talk the young men in the audience frequently interrupted with shouts of "umpah" and the Chief nodded his approval. Thus encouraged, I gave it my all. It seemed to me that they were really into it, and I was very pleased with their reaction.

After my talk, I walked arm in arm with the Chief to the great meeting hall where we were slated to have lunch. After lunch, I was expected to address an even larger group on a different topic. As we walked along, I was all aglow from sniffing the sweet perfume of a successful meeting. While listening to the Chief talk about his plans and programs with one part of my mind, another part was already thinking about my talk to follow. I was deep in thought in the anticipation of a second glorious speech.

Suddenly, the Chief stopped me and steered me sideways and said, "Careful, don't step in the umpah."

It seemed like a safe joke to tell. It fit my theme of not taking oneself too seriously. It should have been okay. In my opinion, I did not belittle or degrade anyone, and I made myself the brunt of the joke. But, it bombed in Wetaskiwin.

Later in my talk, I threw caution to the wind and made another attempt to tell a humorous story. I told the story about one of my friends who was present at this meeting. He was known and well respected by everyone. I told them about another occasion where some of our associates had too much to drink, including our respected friend.

The story goes like this:

Joe, realizing that he had too much to drink, decided to walk home. Rather than take the long way, he took a short-cut through the graveyard. Unfortunately, in the darkness of night, Joe did not see the open hole, and he fell into it. After several attempts to get out, he fell back in a corner exhausted from his unsuccessful efforts. He fell asleep and did not awaken until dawn the next morning. The sun was just casting its first rays of morning. Somewhat confused, having forgotten about the previous night's activities, Joe peered cautiously over the edge. When Joe saw where he was, he muttered "Oh my gosh, judgment day and I'm the first one up.

Nobody laughed. They just stared at me. I don't know, maybe the joke was too close to the truth. Our friend, Joe, was in fact a heavy drinker. For the second time in one evening, *I bombed in Wetaskiwin*.

Socrates said:
"Employ your time improving yourself by other people's writings so you shall come easily by what others have labored hard for."

The reaction of the Wetaskiwin audience—stony-faced silence—reminded me of an experience in high school, when I was in grade 10. Our geography teacher, Mr. Barrows, loved to tell corny jokes. As many as five times during our hour-long class, he would regale us with his brand of humor. Actually, he was quite funny, and he always got giggles from the girls and chuckles from the boys. What I enjoyed the most was the way he laughed at his own jokes.

One day, one of the boys came up with a diabolical idea, and he called a short meeting right before class. His idea was that none of us would laugh until after the girls had their giggles. Then, we would laugh en mass.

It worked perfectly! The joke was told. The girls giggled. The boys sat like statues until the girls were done. Then we laughed loudly. The girls were not in on our little ploy, so this caused them to have another giggle. So, we would laugh once more. At first, Mr. Barrows was confused, so he tried harder to be funny. After the third or fourth attempt, with similar results every time, he got a bit flustered.

Perfect!

Well I wondered if I too had been set up in Wetaskiwin. Since my Wetaskiwin experience, I have never found it easy to find precisely the right humor for a given audience. Since it became politically incorrect to tell certain types of jokes, it is even more difficult.

❧❧❧

There is another version of the graveyard story that I might have told. Perhaps it would have been more successful. I relate it here to illustrate how different endings can be used with the same story:

As before, our buddy Joe was taking a short-cut through the graveyard and fell into the open pit. Poor Joe tried and tried to scramble out of his muddy prison. Each time, he nearly made it, only to slide back in failure. After many attempts, Joe slithered back into a corner, totally exhausted and defeated. Overcome with fatigue, his eyes had just closed when from another corner of the treacherous pit Joe heard, "I knew you could never make it." But he did! This time he made it—first try.

❧❧❧

Forty years ago, when I was a new agent in the life insurance business in London, Ontario, I attended a class on the basics of salesmanship. Our instructor from head office admonished us to refrain from talking about politics, religion, and sex. While he was explaining his point to the group, I packed my books and walked out.

At the door, he stopped me. "Lyle where are you going?"

So I told him. "I can't be a salesman. You just told us to never talk about politics, sex, or religion, and that's all I can talk about."

My associate salesmen laughed loudly and pounded their desks to show their approval.

After the meeting, Jack called me aside to have a little discussion. We knew each other well. Jack had been my boss during the two years I worked in head office.

He said to me, "Lyle, don't you ever do that to me again."

I realized that Jack was chuckling, but he was also serious. It had taken him several minutes to get the program back on track. For the rest of the session, I was a model student. Well, almost!

❧❧❧

A few years ago, my wife and I took my elderly parents to Hawaii for a holiday. My father wanted to see the erupting volcano and my mother just wanted to see Hawaii. During our marvelous holiday, I learned the real value of situational humor.

One day we had a luncheon with some of our friends in the life insurance business. At that time, I was a member of TOP, an acronym for "Top of the Table." Only about 525 sales people in the world qualify each year. So I thought nothing of it when one young man sitting beside me asked lots of questions about how I had qualified for TOP two years in a row.

It seemed to me that Gary had set his sights on going to the top and wanted to learn everything he could. Soon, I discovered that his real motive was to determine if I would make a suitable replacement for Joe Gondolfo.

Joe was a big name in the life insurance business. He was in demand as a speaker. Gary was this year's chairman of the annual conference.

The committee that Gary headed thought they had a contract with Joe. In the eleventh hour, Joe's people demanded two first-class tickets instead of one, four nights in a posh hotel instead of two and double the fee previously thought to have been agreed upon. As you can imagine, the committee was in a quandary.

They had already sold tickets to this event featuring the legendary Joe Gondolfo. Tickets were sold to trust officers and bank managers, as well as to members of the life insurance industry. The bottom line, however, was that the organization could not afford the additional expense. I was flattered to be asked to replace this industry giant, but not for three hours in the morning, a luncheon talk, and two more hours in the afternoon. I agreed to a one-and-a-half-hour keynote. Also, I offered to lead an afternoon discussion on office computerization.

They took me up on the keynote and asked if I would be part of a question and answer panel in the afternoon. Eventually, I learned that I would be sharing the program with Mun Charn Wong and Captain Gerald Coffee. I was thrilled to be billed with these two legends.

Mun Charn had been one of my instructors when I attended the Life Insurance Marketing Institute at Purdue University. Mun Charn is a pulsating star in the life insurance business and a great speaker.

Captain Gerald Coffee is a war hero. He was a naval pilot in the Korean War. His plane was shot down, and he spent the next seven years in prison. Just one year earlier, he had spoken to the Million-Dollar Round Table at a special evening session for the 5,000 attendees. He wowed that audience. At times, you could have heard a pin drop. At other moments, we laughed with gusto. Sometimes, there was not a dry eye in the audience. Captain Coffee took us on an emotional roller-coaster ride.

You can imagine the pressure I felt going into this event, billed along with these superstars. It increased exponentially when I learned that everyone could get a refund if they were not satisfied with the day. I racked my brain for humorous anecdotes and stories.

After my Wetaskiwin experience, I was not going to leave anything to chance. So, for two hours during a meeting with Gary, the evening prior to the event, I ran every bit of humor I could remember through his screening process. Gary laughed continuously, but he rejected each and every story as not suitable for this audience. My speech would be on a high dry plain.

After Mun Charn spoke, I was introduced as the feature speaker replacing Joe Gondolfo. "You have just heard from the teacher. Now you will hear from the student." More pressure! Mun Charn Wong was good, really good, and his talk was witty, gleaning appreciative chuckles from the audience.

As I walked to the front of the room, I could hear birds chirping. There was a slight breeze billowing the curtains. A fan circled lazily overhead. Chairs were scraping, and there was audience noise as they got settled for my talk. Gary was still walking to the back of the room. After greeting the audience with "Aloha," I suddenly turned to Gary and said, "Gary, about my fee."

Gary froze on one foot. The fan stopped, the birds quit chirping, and the curtains stood full at attention. The breeze was stopped dead. The audience sat in stunned silence. Now I was committed, so I continued. I had not planned to do this; it just happened. As the comedian Flip Wilson used to say, "The devil made me do it."

"Gary, I know that we have not had time to discuss my fee, and I think it would be appropriate to do it now."

Nothing could be more inappropriate! Gary was still frozen on one foot, and the audience sat in stunned disbelief at the words they were hearing. Some of them were thinking that I had just committed the biggest blunder any speaker could ever do. I continued: "Gary, I'm sure that you will agree that any speaker worth having is worthy of a fee. Well, I've got a fee, and I want you to know about it now. My fee for today is this. I expect you to write to my head office, Aetna Canada in Toronto, and tell them that you canceled Joe Gondolfo to get me."

The room erupted in laughter. The fan started again. The birds chirped louder than before, and a welcome breeze floated all of the curtains out gracefully. Gary's heart attack was averted, and the mood was set for the rest of my day.

That was spontaneous situational humor. It was risky, but it was appropriate, and that is why it worked. If the audience had not laughed, however, I would have died.

Thinking about this possibility reminded me of the story about Babe Ruth pointing to the bleachers with his bat. Babe Ruth was the most exciting homerun slugger in the history of baseball. In the latter innings of one game, he strode to the plate. The pitcher delivered. The Babe held up one finger. Strike one! The pitcher delivered again. Ruth held up two fingers. Strike two! Then just before the pitcher wound up to throw the next pitch, Ruth gestured to left field, indicating that he would hit a home run. The pitcher fired the ball, and Ruth sent it into the left-field bleachers. Home run!

After the game, a newspaper writer asked Ruth, "Wouldn't you have felt pretty sheepish if you had not hit that home run?"

Ruth glowered at the reporter and said, "That thought never crossed my mind."

Later in my talk, I made a point about our duty as salespeople in the financial world to get people to save and provide for any future financial crisis.

On my way to the meeting, I had tried to stop at a bank to cash a traveler's check. There was a huge lineup of men and women. I did not have time to wait in this lineup, so I proceeded with only the cash in my pocket. I was sure Gary would cover all of my expenses anyway. Later, I learned that people getting their monthly government dole caused the awesome lines. Everyone in the audience nodded knowingly.

At that moment, I was comfortable enough with my audience to attempt a somewhat risky story. These lineups reminded me of a story that was told about our Canadian natives. It goes like this:

A native, walking across an open field, stumbled over a genie bottle. The genie emerged and offered three wishes. Our victim, in this tale, stated immediately that he would like a robin-egg-blue Cadillac. It appeared magically before his very eyes. For his second wish, he wanted to be a man of European descent. And instantly his wish was granted. He now spoke with a distinctly British accent. "Now then, for my third wish, you may make it so I never need to work another day in my life." Poof! He was a Canadian native again.

The audience roared with laughter of approval. I was vastly relieved. During the story, I was conscious of my previous education. I did not want another Wetaskiwin experience. The story worked because of several factors. *It fit the point I was making.* It was situational. I had earned the right by now with this audience to tell a slightly risky story. They knew that it was not my intent to demean any person, neither in Hawaii nor in Canada. The story merely illustrated the point of my talk.

In retelling the story in this book, I am confident that no one will take umbrage with it because I do not tell it disparagingly. Hopefully, no one will read anything into this story other than its value as light humor.

Well, does all situational humor need to be spontaneous? Not at all. However, it does add to the effect. Gary would have rejected the story if I had thought of it the previous evening. I had not planned to tell it. It just happened. "The devil made me tell it." I have never had another occasion to tell it during a talk. The story must fit the situation.

During the afternoon session, I shared the podium with Captain Gerald Coffee. Mun Charn was not able to stay because of other commitments.

The questions asked provided for many occasions of spontaneous hilarity. Sometimes the audience asked Captain Coffee insurance questions. When he finished with his answer, Jerry would turn to me and say, "How did I do, Lyle?"

Several times, I was asked military questions. I would turn to Jerry and ask, "How did I do, Jerry?"

One question for me was, "How do Canadians feel about living in such close proximity to the United States?" I replied, "Do any of you have a big brother?"

When the meeting finished, Jerry and I were given the traditional reward of a lei. We also got a standing ovation—my first one ever. Captain Gerald Coffee gets them all the time. He was not overly impressed, and I remained humble because it occurred to me that mine was due to the fact that I was standing beside a legend.

According to Adlai Stevenson, "Praise is like perfume. It's okay to smell it as long as you don't swallow it."

As we left the meeting to catch our waiting limousine, I suddenly realized that Jerry was no longer wearing his lei. Ours were made with real flowers, and they were hot around our necks. If you have ever been leied in Hawaii you know what I say is true.

I asked Jerry, "What have you done with your lei?"

He pointed to two little elderly ladies sitting in the hotel lobby. One was regally bedecked with Jerry's luxurious lei. The other sat quietly, perhaps envious of her friend. I approached her with my lei and said, "Ah, I've found you. Welcome to the Islands. Here is your lei."

She looked up at me with a sparkle in her eyes and replied, "Oh, I knew I would get one."

Outside, Jerry and I had a chuckle about her reaction.

Laughter is the lotion for the sunburns of life.

There is a sequel to the Captain Gerald Coffee experience, which contains a valid lesson for all of us. Charlie Plumb was shot down and captured by the Viet Cong. He was battered, beaten, and tortured, just like Captain Gerald Coffee.

Someone asked him, "Well Charlie, obviously you didn't die. What happened?"

Charlie replied, "I was taken to a different prison camp and thrown in a cell where I read something on the wall that saved me."

"What did it say?"

Charlie answered, "'Smile, you're on Candid Camera.' I laughed! At that moment, it was the funniest thing I had ever heard, and I laughed for 2,103 days—just short of six years."

"What did you laugh at, Charlie?"

"Well, they'd beat me and I would laugh. They would starve me and I would laugh."

"How could you laugh?"

Charlie smiled, "I was on Candid Camera; what else could I do? It drove those guys nuts."

Okay, so what's the lesson for us? If you lose a big sale or an important speaking engagement, what do you do? Laugh! What else can you do? If someone calls and says, "I'm from the government, and I'm here to help you,"— Laugh! What else can you do? If the tax laws change again, laugh. If the cashier at the hotel where you are staying gets a little snippy when you ask her to change a twenty-dollar bill, remember you are on Candid Camera. When she asks, "How do you want it?" You reply, "Give me two sevens and a six."

Be innovative; be creative; be different. Laugh!

Two years after my Hawaiian experience, I got a call from one of my friends asking if I could come back. This time, it would be to replace Lyle Blessman. Normally, I would jump at the opportunity, but at this particular time I was very heavily committed. (Déjà vu all over again, as Yogi Berra has said.)

This time, the committee thought that Lyle Blessman had accepted their offer. They were shocked with Lyle's counter-offer. Blessman would be a bargain at any price, but it just was not in the budget. So, I advised my caller that I would do it for them on two conditions:

Number 1, call Lyle Blessman and tell him, "No way! We had a deal and we expect you to stick to it. Furthermore, we cannot afford any more than what we offered." Be firm. If I know anything about Mr. Blessman, he will accept it. Anyway, the money you pay him will be given to charity. Tell him that you want to be his favorite charity.

Now if I'm wrong, and Blessman refuses, here is my number 2 condition. I expect you to bill me as the guy you cancel big-name speakers to get. Tell them you had Margaret Thatcher lined up in case I couldn't be there.

It never happened. Lyle Blessman, the gentlemen that he is, accepted their offer.

Spontaneity is a wonderful gift to humor, but it can also be dangerous. It is better to be prepared with "one-liners" or stories that you know to be safe and effective. To do that, you must test them with friends and safe audiences. Safe audiences are ones that will forgive you even if they don't like your anecdote.

Another technique is to relate a story in such a way that, whatever reaction the audience has, it is the correct one. Good speakers continue as though the reaction, or lack of one, was just what they expected. They may be inwardly disappointed, but they do not let it show.

Patricia Fripp, a renowned international speaker says, "Proceed with your talk as though the reaction of the audience was exactly what you expected."

Comedians and masters of one-liners appear to be spontaneous. When Robin Williams delivers his rapid-fire clever comments, it appears as if they just come out of nowhere. He picks up on the comment or question

from the show host and fires away at random. One wonders how he can be so clever and spontaneous. The secret is that his material is very well rehearsed. Robin Williams spent years of obscurity working in small clubs for free. His early attempts at the Improv were rather poorly accepted.

My good friend Bill Clennan, the memory man, is a master of clever repartee. I have heard dozens of his "one-liners." The one that comes to mind at the moment is—well let me set it up first:

Bill and I were in Lethbridge, Alberta, on one occasion, doing our separate things. In fact, neither of us knew that the other would be in Lethbridge. We were staying in hotels at opposite ends of the city. In Lethbridge, that's not very far, in any case. Nevertheless, we agreed to meet at a location featuring a live piano player. When we arrived, the lounge was packed, but we noticed one table with two ladies, four chairs, but only two glasses. We asked the hostess to see if we could join them. She did and we did. As we approached the table, Bill offered his hand and said, "Hi, I'm the perfect stranger." They giggled and the ice was broken. This comment just came to Bill as he walked toward the ladies.

Bill explains that sometimes he has witty comments in his mind that can be pulled out at the right moment, but, depending on the situation, the comment may sound like something he has never said before. "The secret is," says Bill, "you should not use the same quip too often. Keep it fresh and original."

Bill agrees that comedians like Robin Williams are prepared for any situation. However, Bill explained that when you start with a witticism you know you can get on a roll, and sometimes you surprise everyone with your comments, even yourself.

Recently, Bill and I met for lunch at the *Irish Pub* at the Sheraton Eau Claire in Calgary. At one point, there was a loud crash of dishes in the kitchen. Bill threw his hands in the air and exclaimed, "Don't shoot; I'll marry the bitch." Everyone around us laughed. The other patrons, the bartender, the hostess, and the waitresses laughed. It broke up the tension of the moment.

Now, I would never make a comment like that one. First of all, I would not think of it in time. Secondly, it would be too risky for me. Some people can say things and do things that others should never attempt. Unless your personality and style is such that you can carry it off successfully, you should not attempt it. Bill amazes me with the things he can say. He doesn't just get away with it; he revels in it, and the people around react to him in a delightful way. Waitresses treat him like he is a celebrity. Bill expects it, and he gets it. I admire him, and perhaps I'm a little envious, but it's not my style.

After this slightly outrageous comment, I challenged Bill as to the spontaneity of his sudden reaction. He admitted that this was not the first time he had used this phrase. True, it was the only time he had used it in a public situation, and it appeared to be spontaneous.

On the first occasion, Bill was visiting the parents, brothers, sisters, and close friends of his current love. Bill is an incurable romantic, and he is always in love. He has been married four times.

When the noisy crash occurred on this occasion, the expression popped into his mind. Bill's mind raced over the appropriateness of the thought, and then he said it: "Don't shoot; I'll marry the bitch."

Now, Bill was fully aware of his position as a recent addition to this delightful group of friends and relatives. He made a mental calculation, and then he said it. The results were exactly as he expected. This type of comment is true to Bill's personality, and thus for him it worked. Perhaps you, like myself, could not carry it off, and, therefore, we should not attempt it. However, Bill points out that sometimes we are too timid. We have delightfully outrageous thoughts, but we are afraid to express them for fear that someone will take umbrage with the comment. In Bill's philosophy, we should all lighten up a bit.

If you know your audience and an appropriate thought suddenly occurs to you, you should express it. I agree with Bill's sentiments, providing you stay within your personality limits and your comments will not cause pain to anyone.

On one occasion, I introduced Bill at a CAPs meeting (Canadian Association of Professional Speakers) with a poem:

> Our speaker today is a master of seduction,
> And thus my friends, he needs no introduction.
> Therefore, as soon you will see,
> That's one thing this day he'll not get from me.
> However, let me share some little tidbit,
> For I want you to know it before I forget.
> A memorable guy is the memory man,

And I, for my part, am a very staunch fan.
Once I was his mentor, and now he is mine.
Well, considering his stature, to me that's just fine.
He works out there in the school of hard knocks.
That's where he chose to give most of his talks.
Through the years he has grown in wisdom and in knowledge.
He's come a long way since his days spent in college.
Our guest on this day is a speaker, a writer, and a poet,
Whereas, I am not, and it's obvious you all know it.
It's true I am not a Keats, a Longfellow nor even an Edgar Guest.
So before they hear this and wake up from the dead,
I admit the problem is that I made this up in my head.
Oh, what's this dear friends; am I boring you?
If that is the case, let me say without further ado.
Our speaker today is not Chrétien nor Yeltsin nor Lenin,
He is my good buddy—Bill Clennan.

When Bill came up to the podium, I added some information, as instructed. He wanted me to mention that he had given several thousands of talks and made a lot of money. So I asked him, "Bill, is it true that you have given over 2,500 talks throughout Canada, the United States, and Ireland?"

Bill confirmed it.

Then I said, "I understand that you have made several million dollars as a speaker, and I've got a question about that."

Bill nodded, and I continued, "Where did it all go?"

This was totally unrehearsed, and a lesser speaker might have been thrown with this seemingly rude question. Not Bill! Without a moment's hesitation, Bill held up four fingers and said, "Four wives, count 'em—four."

❦❦❦

Sarcastic witticism can be hilarious to some people present, but it may be devastating to the one or ones to whom it is directed. Sarcasm can be a powerful weapon when used in the wrong setting. When Don Rickles, Buddy Hackett, or other comedians like them use this form of humor, it can be very effective. It has no lasting effect because they are not directing it at someone they know.

Sometimes, even the skilled comedians can have a jibe backfire. One evening, Don Rickles picked on a lady from the audience who was badgering him somewhat. If you try to match wits with Don Rickles you're asking for it. And you will get it—rudely.

Rickles turned to this lady, his assailant, and asked, "How much would it cost to get you to haunt a house?"

The lady fired back, "How many rooms?"

❦❦❦

Another speaker I know, Thomas J. Wolfe, CLU, Ch.F.C., had an experience with a heckler. While he was speaking, someone at the back of the room hollered out, "Hey, you're stupid."

Tom was taken aback, but he had been schooled to ignore rude remarks, so he continued on. About two minutes later, the heckler said, "Tom, didn't you hear me—you're stupid."

Again, Tom ignored him and continued with his talk. A third time the heckler shouted, "Hey Wolfe, you're not listening—I said you're stupid."

By now, Tom's patience had worn thin, and he replied, "Listen, I may be stupid, but you're drunk."

The heckler fired back, "I know, but tomorrow I'll be sober, and you will still be stupid."

Some days you just can't win.

❦❦❦

Tom uses humor in selling as well as when he is speaking. Tom says: "Humor is great! It lightens people up. It's a wonderful thing to use, but, of course, it can't be off-color."

Tom is an outstanding salesman and an expert speaker. Getting him wound up is easy. Slowing Tom down is as easy as wrestling a wild steer. Most speakers need to drink water when they speak. Tom needs a lot of water because his throat gets so dry.

One evening, in a client's home, Tom was involved in a long discussion. That evening he was exceptionally dry, and he kept asking his client for a glass of water. Finally, after two hours of explanations and answering questions, Tom asked, "Would you mind getting me one more glass of water?"

His client took the glass and said, "You know, Wolfe, you're the first windmill I've ever seen run by water."

☙☙☙

There is a delightful true story about a well-known international speaker, a lady with a distinctly British accent. On her most recent trip to Calgary, some of her associates took her to Yuk Yuk's. As you may know, many of the comedians use some very colorful language including the "F" word.

One comedian asked the audience to volunteer where they were from. When that person would say the name of the city, the comedian would make a sarcastic comment about it to the delight of the audience. Our associate volunteered, "San Francisco, California." "And what do you do there, little girl?"

She is somewhat diminutive in stature, but she is a giant with verbal repartee. Without hesitation, but with considerable gusto, she replied, "Why I teach people like you to do an entire routine without ever saying F_ _ _."

Can you believe it? This prim and proper lady actually said it in a semi-public place. The shock value was powerful and the audience erupted. The speaker was, appropriately, at a loss for words.

For the remainder of the evening, the comedians who followed would look hesitantly toward the lady from San Francisco before they made any off-color remarks. The audience loved it. Undoubtedly, this spontaneous humor was the highlight of the evening.

Success is a matter of luck. Just ask any failure!

Now I would like to illustrate the value of being prepared. I entered my first speaking contest in grade seven. I came in second. The only other contestant was a girl in grade eight. When I was in grade eight, I won my first contest and went on to regionals, where I placed second. This time, there were eight contestants. In high school, I entered all effective-speaking contests. Our school had four houses, Alpha, Beta, Delta, and Gamma. Each house could enter one contestant for each category. In grade nine, in junior men's, I placed second. In grade ten, I placed second. There seems to be a pattern developing here.

In grade eleven, senior men's, I placed second. But this time, for the first time, I was bitterly disappointed. I knew I should have won. My

Some people are hard of hearing,
but most are just hard of listening!

ten-minute prepared speech was the best, and I delivered it flawlessly. Each contestant had to deliver a second talk—a two-minute impromptu. We were given three minutes to prepare.

When I walked off the stage, glowing with the success of my prepared talk, I was looking forward to the impromptu. I reached into the box and drew a small slip of paper with my topic printed on it, "The funniest thing that ever happened to me." It should have been a piece of cake, but my mind went blank. I could think of nothing. When I walked back on stage and the topic was announced, a titter of anticipation ran through the audience—my peers and teachers. My mind remained frozen. I was in a daze. I could not think of anything funny. I mumbled something and left the stage. Afterwards, I thought of many things I might have said.

Perhaps I could have told them about the time my brothers and I went fishing and camping with our father, in northern Ontario. We were camped on a river with dark brackish water running past. We boiled our water for drinking and for cooking. One morning, while Dad prepared the pancake batter, I boiled the water. Then, when Dad asked if the water was ready, we added boiling water to the pancake batter. You don't need to know much about cooking to know what happened.

Or, I could have told them about the time that one of my classmates threw an ink ball at me. I ducked just in time, and the ink ball sailed into the backside of our French teacher's light green skirt, leaving a rather nasty stain. Miss Ovens walked around all day not realizing what had happened to her skirt.

I could have ended that story with, "But don't worry, Joe Colasanti, I won't tell anyone that it was you who threw that ink ball." I could have said simply, "The funniest thing that ever happened to me was me up here trying to be funny." But I didn't and I placed second.

That day, I learned a valuable lesson. *Be prepared*. I went home and wrote out fifteen two-minute talks. They were structured in such a way that they could fit a variety of topics. At least one of them could be adapted to whatever topic I drew next time. I practised them for a whole year.

In grade twelve, as house captain for the event, I was responsible for getting our contestants—senior men's, senior women's, junior men's, and junior women's. I offered coaching sessions to my associates. Junior men's and junior women's contestants took me up on it. The senior women's contestant declined, and she did not attend any of our sessions. We reviewed our prepared talks and took turns listening to and critiquing each other. I grilled my associates on their impromptu talks. They both prepared several "impromptu" talks. We won! All three of us placed first. The senior women's contestant was second. She did not have a very good impromptu. Some say, "That's cheating." Not so! Not so! It's merely being prepared.

The human mind is a wondrous thing. It begins working the moment you are born, and it doesn't stop working until you stand up to speak!

Situational humor can eliminate tension in nearly any situation. It can change a charged atmosphere and lighten the mood.

A good friend of ours was hospitalized for a second operation. We went to visit him in the hospital. During the first operation, the doctors drilled a hole in his skull and implanted a shunt to draw off excessive fluids. It was successful, but there was a second pocket of fluid causing difficulties.

Again, the doctors drilled a hole in his skull to alleviate the problem. During our visit, after the second operation, Wilf became rather belligerent. That was totally out of character for him. All attempts of our wives to pacify him failed. In fact, their efforts seemed to make things worse. Wilf grew more agitated and was somewhat nasty to both of them. That was totally out of character for him. He would never have acted that way prior to the operation. One of the ladies told him he was being ridiculous.

He turned to me and demanded, "Am I being ridiculous?"

I replied, "Well, you are a bit belligerent, but it's okay. We all know that you've got holes in your head."

Everyone laughed, including Wilf, and a tense situation was averted. Wilf immediately returned to his normal congenial self. Thereafter, whenever Wilf would act even slightly out of character, we would remind him that he had holes in his head. It always worked.

Some years ago, when I was a member of the Windsor, Ontario, Jaycees, I was slated to speak to our assembled members. The speaker before me was a French-Canadian. Our organization was made up of a diverse ethnic membership, which reflected the city's population. You name it; we had it, including Afro-Canadians and French-Canadians.

Pierre spoke with a broad French-Canadian accent. He was very witty. He had our assembled members rocking with laughter. My only problem with this situation was that I was the butt of his humor, and the members loved it. I was not prepared for this. I had no idea that Pierre would make any humorous comments about my character.

I racked my brain for some witty replies. I could think of nothing to say. When it was my turn to speak, I had no rebuttal, and I was resolved to ignore his remarks and just carry on. However, I was fully aware that our associates expected more from me. They expected me to retaliate in kind.

As I looked out at my audience, I saw the look of anticipation in their faces. With a feigned disgruntled look, I faced Pierre and asked, "Pierre, why does Canada have so many French people and the United States so many blacks?"

Pierre replied, "I don't know—tell me."

So I did: "The United States had first choice."

That did it. The audience erupted in raucous laughter. Properly appeased now, I was able to continue with my rather serious talk. We were all friends, and we knew each other well. Those assembled knew that my remarks were meant to disparage neither nationality nor any race. I was simply replying to Pierre's humorous attack on me.

I would not think of telling that story in a different setting. I tell it here only as an example of how situational humor can be effective.

You cannot discover new oceans unless you are willing to lose sight of land.

Two years later, after we moved to Calgary, I did hear that story in a different setting. Shortly after arriving, I joined the YMCA. While sitting in the members' lounge, someone I didn't even know asked me the same question. I pretended I didn't know the answer. It was somewhat amusing because I knew the source of that humor.

Still at the YMCA, but several years later, some friends and I played handball almost every day. Most of the time, Jack, Stan, and I played cutthroat handball. The guy serving literally plays against the other two. It's quite strenuous, and we were serious competitors on the court, with all friendship ignored.

Off the court, we were good friends. So you can imagine my chagrin when one day I walked into the locker room to find my handball buddies going at it nose to nose. At first, I thought they were putting on an act for the benefit of those members standing around. There were no smiles on the faces of the spectators. Suddenly, I realized that these guys were serious, and they were nearly at fisticuffs. I shouldered my way between them. It was like stepping between two fighting dogs. Both dogs could bite you.

Now you need to know that Jack is Jewish and Stan is Polish. We often chided Jack about his membership in a Young Men's Christian Association. We would kid him: "How did you get in? Did you lie at the front desk?"

He would answer, "Yeah, didn't you?"

Jack is head and shoulders taller than Stan. But Stan is pugnacious and a really serious competitor. Now, I found myself between these two bulldogs. Jack snarled at me: "What do you want, Manery?"

I replied: "I've got a question for you. What do you get when you cross a Jew and a Pollock?"

"What?"

"A janitor who owns the building."

The spectators laughed and the tension was dissolved. We proceeded to the handball court, and the argument seemed to be forgotten. They were friends again. In fact, they teamed up to beat me rather badly. I never won a game. So far as I know, the argument never did resume.

Again, let me assure you that no slight was intended to Jewish people, Polish people, or even janitors. It was merely situational humor that broke the tension.

Ironically, a few weeks later, again in the members' lounge, someone asked me, "What do you get...?" "Gee, I don't know."

On another occasion, Stan and I overheard two old guys talking about a friend of theirs who was sleeping with his secretary. I couldn't resist.

I poked my head around the corner and said, "Heck, that's no big deal. I sleep with my secretary every day." Then I added, "Of course, she is my wife."

Stan snapped at me, "Why did you tell them she's your wife. You really had them going." I had to tell, though, because I had more than one secretary, and I didn't want anyone to get the wrong idea. "The devil made me do it." Situational humor!

It was good for a chuckle from all those listening in. But I guess it wasn't all that humorous because no one ever repeated it to me in the members' lounge.

❧❧❧

As I wrote about this incident, I remembered another occasion that runs somewhat parallel to it. Usually, whenever I have a Toronto business trip, I take advantage of it and spend a few relaxing days down on the farm with my parents. On one occasion, some neighbors and long-time friends were visiting. Everyone present was at least twenty years older than I was. My duties quickly became those of a host for the evening. When I returned with a tray of refreshments, I heard our guests discussing marriage vows and some of the people they all knew who were breaking theirs.

Oh, oh, here comes that devil again. I could not resist. With a somewhat serious countenance, I interrupted with a confession: "I know what you mean, my wife has been breaking her marriage vows right from the day we were married."

There was a sudden and perhaps shocked silence.

I explained: "In our marriage vows, Betty agreed to love, honor, and obey me. (That's right, in our vows, it actually says "OBEY.") I continued: "She has never obeyed me yet."

I can still hear my mother cluck, "Oh Lyle—you."

A little timely shock value can provide a humorous moment. Of course, my interruption also ended the other story, and I never did get to hear the juicy details. Who were they talking about anyway?

❧❧❧

One evening, my wife and I went to dinner in a Chinese restaurant. We had just celebrated our thirty-fifth wedding anniversary. We had a lovely young waitress who had recently emigrated from China. We told her that we wanted to visit China. Would she be our guide? She was delighted with the idea. She gave us special attention, and we shared lots of information about ourselves.

We discovered where she was from in China and how and why she came to Canada. She learned about our family and how long we had been happily married.

When the bill came, she handed us our fortune cookies. I asked her if these sayings were true.

She nodded, "Yes, always."

I showed her mine. It said, "You will soon have a new love."

She grabbed it from my hand and proclaimed: "That not for you." She gave me another cookie. It said, "You will be successful in all your endeavors."

She smiled. "Yes, that for you."

❧❧❧

About fifteen years ago, I hired a lovely young lady from India to be my executive assistant. She took over my office and whipped in into shape. Most of our staff was let go, but one, a very industrious conscientious lady, remained with us. She too was from India. Soon after Rani arrived, we packed up the office and moved to a new location. We occupied three floors in the new building. Several months later, we were able to reduce our space requirements to just two floors. That entailed more packing.

In less than a year from that point, I bought part of the building that Rani and I now own. We had to pack up the entire office once again. Rani, Rosmin, her husband, and I worked well past quitting time, packing for the movers who were coming the next day.

Rosmin's husband, Rani, and I were always joking around. Rosmin remained somewhat aloof. She was industrious and conscientious and very prim and proper.

At some point during the evening, Rani commented that she was always packing. She had packed for a move when Manufacturer's Life purchased Dominion Life. Then she packed her office when she joined me. She and her husband had purchased a new home during this time, and she had packed for that move. Now she was packing my office for the third time. She lamented, "I'm forever packing. It seems that all I do is pack, pack, pack."

Without a moment's thought, I replied, "Well, you are a "Packi' aren't you?"

Both Rani and Rosmin's husband exploded in laughter, but Rosmin did not. Rosmin's look could have shriveled an onion. She took me too seriously. Thank the gods of humor that Rani and Rosmin's husband saw my comment as witty. They both knew that there was no malice toward any nationality in my heart nor was anything inappropriate meant by the expressed thought. All of us have chuckled about that expression on more than one occasion since that time. "That devil again. Thanks, Flip."

❦❦❦

About the same time, I was hospitalized with a serious ailment—Crohn's disease. To alleviate my problem, the surgeon "drilled" a hole into my bottom. It left me with a rather tender seating arrangement.

My dear wife made a humorous observation. "It's ironic, you know. You've always been a pain in the ass. Now you've got one."

Ha! She thought it was funny.

After I wrote my book *No Salesman Will Call*, a number of my clients who had read it would say to me, "I thought no salesman would call."

My reply, "Right, I'm the nearest thing to no salesman that my company has got."

One of my female associates gave a number of my books to her clients. When one of them used that line with her, she replied: "That's what it says, but notice it does not say no saleswoman will call."

In that book, I critiqued the writings of over fifty-five authors who wrote about the business I am in without the credentials to do so. When I refer to credentials, I mean education and experience. Their writing proved that they had a serious lack of knowledge and no first-hand experience. Nevertheless, that did not keep them from stating their opinions with authority.

My wife considers it her job to keep me humble. She asked me, "Why are you so hung up on credentials? You've got them; they haven't, but they are the ones making all the money."

Who said, "I would rather be right than President?"

Well, I would rather be right than rich!

When the book was published, I got several speaking engagements to talk about the key issues in the industry, all of which are covered in the book. I closed all of my talks with the following story:

When [an author of financial planning books, for example, like the ones I wrote about] went to see his doctor about pains in his head, they discovered a serious problem. The doctor told him that he had bad news and good news.

"The bad news is that you have an inoperable tumor in your brain. The good news is that we have made such wonderful medical advances recently that we can do a brain transplant with ninety-nine percent safety."

"Wow, how can I get one, and how much will it cost?"

The doctor agreed, "Let me make an appointment for you with a surgeon."

The surgeon directed the patient to a special room that contained a variety of brains. He started off with a lawyer's brain. "Now this one would cost you $2,500."

"That's not bad, with a legal brain I could understand all of the proceedings in parliament."

Next, he moved to an accountant's brain. "This one would cost $3,500."

"Hey, that's even better. Afterwards, I could understand our copious tax laws and the complicated return forms. I like that. $3,500 might be a bargain."

On through the display they went until they got to the brain of an author of financial planning books, like those I wrote about. Almost with reverence, the surgeon explained that this one would cost $100,000.

"Wow," exclaimed the patient, "I can understand $2,500 for a lawyer's brain and $3,500 for an accountant's brain. But how can you justify $100,000 for the brain of an author of financial planning books?"

"That's easy," replied the surgeon, "It's never been used."

There is humor in incongruity! There are several versions of that story floating around. I did not originate it. But my version of it illustrates my point precisely. This anecdote has worked every time so far. It works because it fits my topic and I know my audience.

That story demonstrates another point. Many speakers say that you should never use someone else's story. I agree. If a speaker is using a particular story or analogy, you should not undermine him or her by using the same one. Imagine following someone on the podium that has just used all of your favorite stories. It happens.

On the other hand, if you can take an old tale that is not being told by another speaker (so far as you know) and revise it so it is not recognizable as someone else's story, then go for it.

Some professional speakers caution that, if your original story becomes well known, you should stop telling it. However, I have found that enough people in any audience will not have heard the story, and they will laugh. Even those who have heard it will enjoy hearing it again, and they will laugh because the majority of the audience is laughing. Most people cannot remember a punch line for half an hour, let alone twenty-four hours. There is one lady in my acquaintance to whom I can tell the same story several times, about one week apart. She laughs every time. I love her.

Anyway, if the story really is your story, it will be obvious to most people hearing it because it fits so well. If it makes your point, who cares if the audience has heard it before?

ぴぴぴ

A case in point: One of my favorite stories relates very well to my estate-planning program. Unfortunately, it also relates to golf. Since I have been telling it during my training sessions, some of my golfing buddies have been relating the story to me. I have no intention of giving it up because it fits my program so well. It goes like this:

Some time ago, I held a session on estate planning for some life insurance sales people. They were allowed to bring their clients to the session at no cost. In my program, I teach that couples, and sometimes even families, should discuss all aspects of their financial planning. This should be done in detail, and that's why the family can be involved— benefiting all.

A few days after one session, one of my associates came to me and said:

Guess what happened. The couple that was with me, my clients Bob and Norma, took your advice to heart and followed your directions carefully. As instructed, Bob and Norma discussed their plans, desires, and wants in some detail. They recorded their reasons for certain decisions exactly as had been recommended.

After making all the big decisions about their prior-to-death and their post-death wants and desires, they got around to discussing some rather more personal matters. Bob asked his wife, "If I die first, will you remarry?"

After a reflective moment, Norma answered, "Well, I probably would. Psychologists claim that people who have had happy marriages are at least twice as likely to get married again. So based on our wonderful marriage, the answer is 'yes' definitely I would marry again."

Bob nodded sagely and asked, "Would you and your new husband live here, in our house?"

Norma answered thoughtfully, "Yeah, I imagine we would. I mean, I really like this area of the city. The neighbors are great and, furthermore, this house is paid for, and it's fixed up just the way I want it."

"Okay," Bob commented, "but would you let him use the recreation room in the basement that I worked so hard to finish during the past three years?"

Slightly exasperated Norma replied, "Dear, you cannot possibly think that I could let my new husband live here in this house and make some rooms out of bounds." Softening a little, she said, "You wouldn't want me to enshrine the rec room as a monument to you, would you?"

Bob shook his head pensively, "Well no, of course not. That's silly of me to even mention it. But there is one other thing I am concerned about."

"What's that dear?" Norma asked.

"Well," Bob continued, "Would you let him use my $2,000 set of golf clubs?"

"Heavens no, Bob;" retorted Norma, "he's left-handed.

Another agent told me about his experience with a couple discussing what would happen after death. The wife kept on her husband about what he would do if she died first. Finally, somewhat flustered, he decided to put a stop to this line of questioning. He said, "Yes dear, I'd marry another women just like you were—a blonde nineteen-year-old."

She snapped back at him, "Forget it, I'm going to outlive you anyway."

❧❧❧

Previously, I mentioned that my wife has appointed herself to keep me humble. She took over the job from my mother. Mother always knew when to puncture the bubble to keep her sons from floating off into space. She also seemed to know the precise moment to add a little boost to the old ego. For example, in my case, knowing that I was not particularly handsome, Mother would often say something to bolster my confidence. After I finished dressing nervously for the prom or a first date, she would say, "My, you look handsome."

Thinking back, it was never, "You are handsome." It was always "You *look* handsome."

❧❧❧

Down on the farm, up on the farm, out on the farm, wherever it is, there are always lots of chores to do. I was the eldest of four boys, and it seemed to me that Mother always said, "Lyle, will you get this?" Or "Lyle, will you do that."

I used to wonder if she couldn't remember my brothers' names. I put a list of their names on the cupboard door over the stove, with my name at the bottom. She still called my name first. I left my name off the list. That did not work either.

So, one day, I complained, "Mom, every time there is a chore to be done, you ask me to do it. Why do you always tell me to do it? Can't you tell one of the others to do it?"

She looked at me with a slight frown, "Well, I could, but if I ask you, I know it will get done right."

Oops! I never complained again. Where did she learn to be a psychologist? Obviously, it came from raising four farm boys.

❧❧❧

When I graduated from university in psychology, I occasionally used some words that were not part of my mother's regular vocabulary. She would bring me up smartly with, "Don't think we sent you to college so you could use words we don't know. If you learned anything at all, you should have learned words that we all know to express your ideas."

Naturally, after this lecture, I looked for words that might annoy her a little, just to hear her rail at me. Sometimes when she did, I would tell her that I was just repeating what my brother Grant said. If Grant said it, it was okay then. He graduated as an electrical engineer.

❦❦❦

Recently, we visited my mother, who lives 2,200 miles from us. She is now age 86 and as feisty as ever. While there, she asked me what I was working on now. Taking a phrase from Earl Nightingale, I told her I was trying to become a *postprandial ululator*.

She just rolled her eyes back a bit and said, "Humph, I always did think you were a bit touched."

For those who do not know the meaning of these words from Earl Nightingale, I will save you the trouble of looking them up. "Postprandial" means "after a meal" or "after dinner." According to Nightingale, "ululator" refers to "a howling monkey." Hence the phrase means—"After-dinner speaker."

❦❦❦

While visiting Mother on this occasion, we sat down to review her financial situation. This was the first opportunity we had to do so since my father had died. After looking everything over, I tried to reassure her that she was in good financial shape to at least age 120.

Mom looked at me seriously and asked, "Then what?"

❦❦❦

Family meals at our farm were fun times when we were all home. After a meal, we liked to sit around with our coffee and tell tall tales. Dad always enjoyed good humor, and you could count on him to laugh the loudest. It was a joy to hear his explosive laugh, so we all told our best stories whenever we were home.

One of the funny asides was when, as often happened, after everyone had stopped laughing, my sister-in-law would exclaim, " I don't get it!"

This would cause another chuckle, and still another followed when my brother Woody would say, "Never mind; I'll explain it to you later."

One day, Woody remained stony-faced and puzzled while everyone else laughed. Then he exclaimed, "I don't get it."

Instantly, my sister-in-law fired at him, "Never mind; I'll explain it later."

The ability to laugh
is one of God's great gifts to human beings.

Dad loved to laugh at other people's jokes, but he rarely attempted to tell one himself. He was more apt to relate exploits about his hunting and fishing buddies. Ever heard of buck fever? You don't catch it; you get it when you see a big buck elk coming right at you with a rack of horns as big as the grill on a Mack truck and flared nostrils that would swallow your fist and arm right up to your elbow. If you were one of the boys from the hunting camp, you might have to listen while Dad regaled the assembly with your weakest moments as a great white hunter.

Dad became a camera buff in later years and found ways to use it to provide a little hilarity. One day, he decided to put an end to the snickering when he told about "the one that got away." He set the scene like a movie director. Dad stood on a rock about ten feet above the river, with his fishing rod bent over in a great arch.

Another of his cronies was set to push a huge rock into the river to create an awesome splash. The camera was arranged to capture both the splash and Dad with his fishing rod stretched to the breaking point. The picture was perfect.

After that, whenever someone would tell about the one that got away, Dad would produce his photo of "the" one that got away. "One picture is worth...."

While Dad didn't often tell jokes, he nevertheless did have a keen sense of humor. A few years before Dad's death, we went bass fishing in my new boat. While I was getting the motor set to idle and getting us into a good spot to fish, Dad got his rod ready and his lure in the water.

By the time I was prepared to start, Dad was already trolling. As soon as my line was out, Dad asked, "$1 for the first fish?"

I replied, "Sure, let's do it!" I always enjoy a sporting venture.

With a wry grin, Dad said, "Pay me." His lined was bowed already with the first fish of the day.

❧❧❧

Well, I have mentioned two of my brothers, Grant and Woody (Elwood), so I'll mention my youngest brother, Neil. "Hi Neil."

Neil married a French-Canadian lady, Michelle. To this day, Michelle speaks English with a delightful French-Canadian accent. I love to mimic her.

On one of our visits to Ottawa, Michelle accompanied my wife and me and our two sons to see the parliament buildings. For the guided tour, there were two lines—one for French-speaking and one for English-speaking visitors. The francophones got to go first. We waited!

Michelle was at the head of our line. Behind her was my family, and following us were English-speaking visitors from other parts of Canada and the United States.

In a clear voice, with her solid French-Canadian accent, Michelle announced, "It is too bad that the rest of you don't speak French; then we could get to go first too."

My family exploded in laughter, but the remainder of the line was not too sure about this form of humor—in this place, at this time. Michelle was quite serious, but to me it was just funny. If I had thought of it first, I would have said it, using my mimic of Michelle's accent. I could have blamed Flip Wilson's devil.

❧❧❧

On one occasion while I was visiting in Ottawa, Michelle learned that I was on my way to Montreal. She said, "You know, Lyle, while you are in Montreal you should take my sister, Janine, out to dinner." Janine is a younger sister.

I told her, "I would be delighted to take her to dinner."

Michelle telephoned her sister and set it up. Then she handed the phone to me and said that I should discuss it with Janine. We talked for about five minutes, and we agreed to meet for dinner on Thursday.

Just before we ended our conversation, Michelle said, "Let me talk to her again. She took the phone from me and said, "Remember, Janine, he is a married man."

We live in a world of contradictions.
Consider these oxymorons:
Jumbo shrimp, civil war, postal service.

There are some situations that warrant a story's inclusion in this book even though it has surfaced elsewhere. Let me give you an example.

Nearly fifty years ago, when my brothers and I were still down on the farm, an incident occurred that we found amusing. At noon, we all came in from the field ravished with hunger. As always, Mom had prepared a great meal. (See below for a definition of Mom's great cooking.)

We were too hungry for small talk, and in too much of a rush to get back outside "to make hay while the sun shines." Mother, on the other hand, had been alone all morning, doing her thing for her husband and her four sons. She wanted some conversation.

However, if you have ever watched piglets at the slop trough, you may get a better vision of what we were like. We were focused. We had one goal—FOOD. There was no time for niceties. Can it keep until dinner? Nope!

Mom wanted some reaction from us. I can hear her to this day. "Boys, I don't think your dad loves me. We've been married for eighteen years, and he never tells me he loves me."

We did not ignore her. We merely followed her previous admonition, "Don't talk with your mouth full."

Finally, Dad scraped back his chair, and as he left the table he said, "Woman, I told you I loved you when I asked you to marry me. If anything changes, I'll let you know."

Over the years, I've told that true story many times. One day, a young lady listening exclaimed, "Oh, Lyle, you read that in *Reader's Digest*." I did not! Furthermore, I did not authorize anyone to put my story in that magazine.

This also illustrates another point. It is possible for the same original humor to surface at different times in different places. After all, a similar humorous situation may occur more than once. In my mind, I have created lots of things that I later discovered already existed. *Some people say that if a story gets published, even if it is your story, you can't use it any more.* Nonsense! If it fits the conversation, use it.

ଙଙଙ

Now, about Mom's great cooking. A number of my friends have told me that the memory of their mother's great meals is better than the reality. In other words, years later, Mom doesn't cook as well as you remember. Perhaps when you were young and constantly hungry you thought she was a really great cook. Maybe she was, or maybe you enjoyed it so much because you had little else for comparison. I cannot agree entirely. Many women in our neighborhood could bake great pies. We ate them at shredding bees, but my mom's were still the best.

I think my mother's explanation is accurate. According to her, she used to be a better cook when she prepared large meals. Now, after years of cooking and baking for only two people, she is not as good as she once was. Maybe so, but her meals are still very tasty. Food down on the farm is still mouth-watering good to me.

ଙଙଙ

My son Darryl has a well-developed sense of humor. He seems to have acquired it from his Uncle Jay—my wife's brother. Jay is constantly coming out with witticisms that bring chuckles or groans from those around him. For example: "If you fly around the world, at what point will you be flying upside down?"

If Darryl were present when Jay proffered his question, Darryl might reply, "You don't—in modern planes you just fly high enough to sit there while the earth turns under the plane." Groaner!

Jay likes to come out with things like:

- Friends, Romans, countrymen—lend me your ears. On second thought, lend me your wallets. What good is a bushel of ears, unless it is corn?
- Do you ever run out of work? Then slow down to a walk.

- Don't give your wife all the credit—give her some cash once in a while.
- I believe we are going to get some weather—the sky is in the north.

Does Jay use these and other sayings over and over? Well, does a chicken lay eggs? Does a fifty-pound bag of flour make a biscuit? Does a bear...? Darryl and Jay, together in one room, are too much.

❦❦❦

Not all humor needs to elicit laughs that come from one's lower stomach area. A good joke is quite effective even if it only elicits a groan. An actor portraying a fumbling comedian in a TV program explained it. This "comedian" was trying to demonstrate his humor to a jury. His ex-wife was suing him for using her lines. She was a professional writer for comedians. Her lines were clever, witty and funny. His were not humorous; rather, they were a bit caustic. The jury was not amused.

During a short intermission to allow the lawyer to get his client under control, the comedian implored his lawyer to let him continue. He stated, "They (the jury) don't have to laugh out loud. I know they are breaking up inside." They were not.

However, there is a point here. *Some humor can be subtle*. It can titillate your intellect. Some people may smile or chuckle, but for some it may cause only an eye twinkle. They appreciate it, but it does not elicit a tear-jerking response. Some of the best humor is merely mental stimulation. Of course, as the comedian said, sometimes it can be so subtle that the full impact does not hit until some time later. About the jury, he said, "They will wake up at 2:00 a.m. thinking about it. They may not be able to go back to sleep right away because of the thought stimulation caused by the witty remarks."

❦❦❦

When my son Darryl was emcee at a wedding reception for one of his best friends, we experienced the power of subtle humor. The bride's friends and relatives outnumbered the groom's support group by about three to one. They did not know what to expect from Darryl. For that matter, neither did we. No question, we knew that Darryl liked to tell stories and make comments to cause his friends to laugh.

Actually, when we were entertaining friends, Darryl, about six years old, thought it was his duty to aid us with some schoolyard humor. To avoid being embarrassed, we would not let him continue until his older brother Scott listened privately and gave his approval. Scott, like his mother, has good sense when it comes to what is acceptable and what is not. As Scott used to edit Darryl's humor, his mother now edits mine. (Admittedly, she has not approved of some of my attempts at humor in these pages.)

On one occasion, we were summoned by Darryl's grade two teacher to help her with a problem. It seemed that Darryl was apt to make witty comments that stimulated laughter from his classmates. Sometimes this happened during her most serious moments. Were Darryl's comments rude or crude, sarcastic or naughty? "No, not really. They were just witty at inappropriate moments." *Indeed, what is humor if it is not an appropriate comment at an inappropriate time?*

Unlike his teacher, I did not see this as a problem. I suggested to her that she might be able to take advantage of the situation. Use Darryl's observations to illustrate the point of her discussion. Reply to his humor with an equally witty comment of her own. Turn the tables on Darryl with some good-natured humor. As I saw it, she had a great opportunity to add some interest to her classroom. After all, six hours of classroom work, five days a week, can become a little boring to young minds. Certainly, I respected her need to control her classroom, but curtailing a natural talent, a gift of one of her students, was not the best way to deal with it. I encouraged her to avoid destroying Darryl's natural talent.

On the occasion of his first attempt as a wedding emcee, Darryl's humor surprised everyone, including his mother and me. For starters, Darryl provided a number of humorous insights into Kevin's life-style as a bachelor. One, for example, was about Kevin's dishwashing habits.

Darryl framed a sprinkler head, which he presented to Kevin with the comment, "You will not need this now. I'm sure that you will not be tossing your dishes on the lawn to be sprayed-clean anymore."

Darryl regaled the guests with a story about his long-term relationship with Kevin. "We go way back as friends, even back to fetus-hood. You see we were in the womb at the same time."

"Well, not the same womb. We each had separate wombs."

"Kevin was always kicking for more space. Having a waterbed of his own and personal maid service was not enough. He also wanted a womb with a view."

Darryl continued, "Kevin was evicted before me, but eventually we were both evicted." At this point in the narration, an uncle of the bride piped up, "Did you get back your damage deposit?" This brought gales of laughter from the guests.

Darryl's retort was equally hilarious, "Oh no, we didn't get the damage deposit back because our fathers' made the initial deposits."

Afterwards, I challenged Darryl with the thought that he and the bride's uncle had set it up. He assured me that it was not planned. I approached the uncle with the same accusation. He was adamant that it was not planned—it was spontaneous.

☙☙☙

Darryl's performance as wedding emcee was the highlight of the reception, and he had not even heard of Brian Lee's book, *The Wedding MC*. I wonder how much better he might have been if he had studied Brian's classic. Brian Lee, CSP, a leader in the Canadian Association of Professional Speakers, is a font of knowledge for speakers and writers. Brian's success story is awesome. It happened overnight, after sixteen years of intensive study and work. Actually, Brian's background in business and in politics prepared him very well for his career as a professional speaker.

For the past three years, Brian has been my mentor, and I am grateful for the many things he has taught me. Brian is an author of several books, training courses, and workshop programs. In addition to his professional speaking activities, Brian is a coach to would-be speakers.

On the subject of humor, Brian advised me that a good rule to follow is, "Can you tell it in church?" That is good advice.

Well, I thought I was safe when I repeated a story about a Southern Baptist minister. During his inspirational talk to the over five thousand attendees at one of our annual Million Dollar Round Table conferences, this minister admitted that sometimes a Baptist congregation could be a little overly strict.

He stated, "I know people in our congregation that would never make love standing up for fear that someone would see them and think they were dancing." His comment brought the house down. Have you ever heard five thousand people in one room laugh? *This was an appropriate comment from a seemingly inappropriate source.*

Well now, following Brian's advice—"If you can tell it in church..." I felt comfortable telling the story anywhere. After all, my source was no less than the inspirational leader of a large Southern Baptist church congregation.

I related the story to some of my seriously religious friends and relatives. They did not see it as humorous. In fact, they were slightly embarrassed. They did not laugh. Obviously, I had misjudged my audience. Brian's advice is correct, but there is another adage that should be remembered: "Know your audience."

The Baptist minister's comment was appropriate to his talk to his audience on a special occasion. When I related it, it was simply not appropriate to my smaller audience. When I told the story, I was not making a point, and it came across as criticism of all people who were opposed to dancing as a social activity.

Well, I'm not easily deterred merely because the assembled group doesn't appreciate my brand of humor. Just like the deluded comedian described earlier, I knew they were secretly chuckling inwardly. They would laugh out loud later that night, no doubt.

❧❧❧

So I told them a few more stories about pastors and ministers. The first one was about a minister who decided to hold his regular Sunday-morning sermon outside in the fresh air. Sunday morning came, and it was a gloriously warm sunny morning. An old farmer living near the church had offered to set things up for this meeting in the open. He placed bales of straw to serve as a platform for the preacher and surrounded them in a semicircle with bales of hay for the congregation to sit on. When the preacher arrived, the old farmer was sitting on his rail fence. No one else was present. They waited. Nobody else showed up. They waited.

Finally, the preacher said, "Well, if you went out to feed your cattle and only one cow showed up, would you feed her anyway?"

"Yes, I would," allowed the farmer.

Thus encouraged, the preacher proceeded to proclaim his message for the next hour. Afterwards, as speakers and preachers are wont to do, he looked for a little feedback from the congregation. The old farmer complied, "Reverend, if I was to go out to feed my herd and only one cow showed up, I would give her nourishment all right, but I wouldn't give her the whole load."

Well, Brian, I would tell it in church, but with my friends and relatives, it didn't receive too much enthusiasm on this occasion. Well, they did chuckle just enough to encourage my next attempt.

❦❦❦

One day a new minister arrived, and he decided to survey his parish. He drove for miles throughout the countryside appraising its potential. He would meet the parishioners later with some knowledge of their whereabouts.

He was learning a great deal about them just looking at the farms, the houses, and the farm buildings, barns, granaries, silos, and so on. The new minister drove past one farm several times. He was very impressed with its appearance. It was neat and tidy. The farmhouse was very impressive, so clean and friendly-looking. The farm buildings were freshly painted and appeared to be in great shape. The land was well tilled. Neither a stray weed nor an obstructive rock could be seen.

The minister noticed that the farmer was there in one field on his tractor. He waited at the end of one nicely cultivated row. When the farmer arrived, he got down off his tractor to meet the stranger. After introductions all round, the minister said, "Well, you must feel truly blessed to have such a wonderful farm."

The farmer, a Scotsman, replied, "Aye, I surely do."

The minister continued, "I cannot help noticing the well-kept buildings, and the beautiful fields with the luxuriant crops. You must feel the blessings of our Lord."

The farmer agreed, "Aye, aye, that I do."

The minister continued in the same vein ending each time with, "You must be so thankful with this bounteous gift from God."

Finally, the farmer looked straight at the minister and said, "Preacher, I have told you that I am thankful and all that, but let me tell you, you should have seen it when he had it all to himself."

That brought a slight tremor from those assembled, so I tried again.

❦❦❦

A young preacher, in his new parish went to the senior pastor for some advice. He stated, "I'm having the hardest time on Sunday morning. I can't get the congregation to pay attention to me.

They show me no respect. I get up to preach, and they just keep on with fellowship activities, and discussing the Sunday school lesson from the Bible."

The old preacher said, "I understand. I had that trouble one time. You just get up there and make a startling opening statement."

The young preacher asked, "What statement did you use when you had this trouble?"

The older man chuckled, "One Sunday, they wouldn't get quiet, so I rapped on the pulpit and said right down to them, 'Some of the most favorable moments in my life have been spent in the arms of another man's wife.' In church, young man, they will look right up at you and you can hear a pin drop. They'll drop those Bibles and pay attention. Now, young man, you've got to remember one thing. Before the sermon is concluded, you be sure to tell the congregation that the other man's wife to whom you referred earlier was your mother."

The young preacher chuckled, "I think that would work for me." The following Sunday, he was anxious to try it out. In they came, and they didn't get quiet. Taking his mentors advice, the inexperienced preacher rapped on the pulpit and said, "Some of the most pleasurable moments in my life were spent in the arms of another man's wife."

At this juncture, his tiny redhead wife leapt out of her pew, about seven rows back and went storming up the isle. Her eyes were flashing, and her face was red as a beet.

Seeing her in this state, the young preacher got all flustered and mixed up. He babbled, "And for the life of me, I can't remember who it was."

❦❦❦

Isn't that good? I looked around me and noticed that I was the only one laughing. So, after a moment, trying to recover, I told them another one:

An old preacher lived next door to one of his parishioners. They were always visiting back and forth over the fence. One day, the layman neighbor had his car jacked up, changing a flat tire. When the jack slipped and fell, the layman said, 'Well, I'll be damned."

The preacher admonished him. "Don't say things like that. The next time something of that nature happens, just say 'Praise the Lord'."

The layman neighbor, slightly embarrassed, replied, "I'll watch that next time, Preacher; I promise you, I will."

Well, about six weeks later, he had the car jacked up again, and he was down under it working on the car when the jack slipped and the car fell pinning him under it. The old preacher was watching in shock. From under the car came the words, "Praise the Lord." The car lifted right up. And the stunned preacher said, "I'll be damned."

Well, I still did not get the response I wanted from this group, so I decided to follow another advisory from Brian. *Get another audience.*

☙☙☙

I am truly impressed with Brian Lee and his twin brother Bruce, not merely because of their success as international speakers, although I admit that they are both very accomplished in their chosen fields. But what impresses me most is the story about one of their ancestors— Great-great-great-grandpa General Lee:

Now, you should not be confused about which general I refer to. You see, I do not allude to Charles Lee, who was an American general in the revolutionary war. I do not refer to Henry Lee, who was known as 'Light horse Harry Lee.' He, also, was a general in the revolutionary war. Nor do I refer to Henry's cousin, Richard Lee, American revolutionary statesman and signer of the Declaration of Independence. Furthermore, you should not assume it was Robert Edward Lee, Commander-in-Chief of the Confederate army in the Civil War. These men may be illustrious ancestors, but this is not their story.

When Great-great-great-grandpa Lee graduated from Yale University, he joined the army. He applied to be a general. Well, at that time, the army needed all the generals they could get. During the war, generals did not survive too well. However, this ambitious young man had no experience. Simple solution, they hired a Prussian general to teach the basics to Great-great-great-grandpa General Lee. Before training was complete, however, they were faced with the imminent prospects of a battle. In fact, one morning they discovered the enemy lined up only a few thousand yards away. They were armed with bayoneted rifles ready to strike. The Prussian general, seeing this, instructed his 'aide de camp' to fetch his red tunic.

Great-great-great-grandpa General Lee exclaimed, "My God, Pruss, you'll be a target in the bright red tunic."

The Prussian general replied stoically, "If I am wounded, I don't want my men to see me bleed and then become demoralized."

Now, Great-great-great-grandpa General Lee was no slouch. He was a quick learner—graduate of Yale, no less. He summoned his 'aide de camp,' who was nearby polishing boots. He instructed, "Fetch my dark brown trousers."

Take your time! Think about it. You will probably wake up at two a.m. howling with laughter. I can hear my sister-in-law saying, "I don't get it." That's okay; maybe Woody will explain it.

ಠಠಠ

Sometimes we take ourselves too seriously. Perhaps we need to lighten up a bit. After all, even St. Thomas Aquinas found the use of humor appropriate. He is one of the deepest thinkers I have ever tried to read. When St. Thomas was asked what God was doing before he brought together all the materials to make heaven and earth, he reportedly replied, "He was preparing hell for all those who asked that question."

Did he use a little humor to avoid answering the question?

On the other hand, maybe he was serious about it. I think he saw the humor in his answer. Nevertheless, it does illustrate that sometimes we can use humor to deflect a question that we can't answer. It may be politically unwise to answer a question that catches you in the middle of a disputable topic such as pro-life and the right to decide. No matter how you answer such a question, one group will disagree with you.

ಠಠಠ

Robert Benchley, an American actor and humorist, would answer some questions of this nature by saying, "I'm glad this question has come up, in a way, because there are so many different ways to answer it that one of them is bound to be right."

In the *Speakers Idea File*, Gary Apple suggests, "Someone in the audience asked me that question just last week. And I'm going to dodge it the same way I did then."

George Burns said:
"The most important thing about life is honesty and integrity. If you can fake that, you've got it made.

Cavett Robert, known as the dean of speakers during his lifetime, used to relate a humorous reply made by a politician during the days of prohibition. Cavett explained:

> The editor of a local newspaper had the unmitigated gall to ask a politician how he stood on the whisky question. What a horrible thing to do to anyone, especially someone running for an elected office. You see you be damned if you do and you be damned if you don't. If you are for whisky you get half of the votes and you lose half of the votes. If you say "I am against whisky," you will lose half and you will get half. No matter which way you turn, you are in a bad, bad way. Well this politician acquitted himself in an admirable way.

According to Cavett Robert, this is what the politician wrote:

> Sir, I had not planned to discuss this controversial question at this time. But, far be it from me to sidestep any issue regardless of the nature, regardless of the results.
> But I want to be sure I understand you now.
> If, Sir, when you say whisky you mean that devils brew, that poisonous scourge, that bloody monster of society that defies elegance, dethrones reason, creates misery and poverty and takes the bread from the mouths of babes; if when you say whisky you mean that vile drink that topples the Christian man and woman from the pinnacles of righteous and gracious living into the bottomless pit of despair, deprivation, shame, hopelessness and helplessness, destroys homes, creates orphans

and depraves the community in general; Sir, if that is what you mean by whisky, I call for you to put in your paper that I promise my constituents, if I am elected, I'll fight to destroy this demon with all the strength that I possess.

BUT–

If on the other hand when you say whisky, you mean that oil of conversation; if you mean that philosophic wine and ale that contributes to well being when friends and fellows get together with a song in their hearts, a laugh on their lips, warmth in their eyes; Sir, if you mean that medicinal spirit that puts a spring in the old man's steps on a frosted morn; if you mean that nectar of the gods, the sale of which puts untold millions into our treasury, puts insurance on the family, builds roads and byways, then, Sir, you'll have to admit that there is not a better place to live. Now, Sir, if that's what you mean by whisky, I ask that you put in your paper, 'I'll fight to protect this essence of divinity with all the strength I possess.'

According to Cavett, he added a crowning climax that capstones it all. He said:

Sir, now that I have answered your query without equivocation, I hope that you will in all good conscience put in your paper that I am a man of my convictions.

This is my stand.
I will not compromise.
This is my stand!

❧❧❧

Motion pictures often provide some of the best humor. Sometimes the reaction of the audience can be even funnier than the plot. When I was a freshman in university, the first week was known as "frosh week."

There were many orientation events to help us get to know each other and a bit about campus life. We all wore ridiculous beanies and the men had to walk around with one pant leg rolled up knee high.

This dress style allowed us to recognize each other and to be recognized by upper-class students.

Mild hazing was permitted.

One of the events was a trip to the local movie house. Some sort of love story was playing. I don't remember much about it. But I do remember that the members of the audience made humorous or witty comments throughout. It all started during a tender love scene. The young couple on the screen was standing close, looking dreamily into each other's eyes, but they were not touching. Some guy shouted out, "Kiss her."

That did it. From that point onward, the tender love story became a comedy because of one witty irreverent comment after another.

ช่ช่ช่

Dr. John Powers is a motivational speaker. When he talked to us at a Million Dollar Round Table meeting, he said, "If you can save people time, you can make a lot of money. That's why people go to video stores for tapes of movies."

Dr. Powers told his audience that he and his wife frequently entertained neighbors and friends in their home. One weekend, he and his wife invited an Hispanic neighborhood couple to view two movies with them.

The first one was "West Side Story," which they had all seen previously. At one point, the Hispanic guy piped up. "This is my favorite part. Here a guy is running down the street in an all-Hispanic neighborhood yelling 'Maria' and only one woman ever comes to the window."

Later, they viewed "Indecent Proposal." As you may know, Demi Moore and Woody Harrelson go to Las Vegas where they proceed to lose all their money. A wealthy guy, played by Robert Redford, offers the destitute guy one million dollars if he could spend one night with this lovely wife. The question is, "Will this woman go to bed with Robert Redford for one million dollars?"

At some point during the agonization, Dr. Power's wife exclaimed, "That's a tough call. If they wanted to make a great movie, they should have given the wealthy guy's part to Danny Devito." Movies usually reflect society's need for an escape from reality, and so does the use of humor.

Here is a definition of humor I like:
"Quick to perceive the ludicrous."

George Bernard Shaw said: "The reasonable man [or woman] adapts himself [or herself] to the world: the unreasonable man [or woman] persists in trying to adapt the world to himself [herself]. Therefore, all progress depends on the unreasonable man [woman]." It is obvious, if you can portray a somewhat unreasonable situation in an irreverent manner, you will probably elicit a humorous reaction.

Here are some examples of irreverent humor:

When one insurance agent encounters a proposal that advocates replacing his client's permanent plan with "term and invest the difference," he asks, "Where did this 'fella' tie his horse? When Jessie James tried to pull off a job like this, he always rode a horse."

Three old codgers were bragging about their ugly wives.

One said, "My wife is so ugly, her face would stop an eight-day clock."

The second one stated, "My wife is so ugly, men turn their heads when she walks by—away."

The third guy replied, "Well, my wife is so ugly that one night when she was undressing a peeping tom reached in and closed the blind."

"Beauty is only skin deep, but ugly cuts all the way to the bone."

Surveys have shown that the number one thing that people get depressed about is their own looks. Turn to the person on your left and say, "Your the best looking person I have ever seen."

After a moment, turn back and say, "I was just kidding."

Three other men were also discussing their wives. The first one said, "My wife tells me I'm so distinguished I look like a diplomat."

The second said, "Yeah, my wife tells me I'm so intelligent—I'm the best read man she has ever met."

"My wife is proud of me, too," said the third. "Every time a delivery man comes to the door she announces, "My husband's home! My husband's home!"

One third of the people in the world are ugly. Look at the person on your left, then at the one on your right. If they are both okay ... well.

In college, one of my psychology professors said it slightly differently. "One third of the people in the world suffer from some form of mental illness. Take a moment to check out the person on your left, then the person on your right. If they both seem okay ... well."

A John Wayne-type cowboy spoke to a librarian: "Ma'am can you tell me where I can find the new book '*Man, The Superior Sex*'?"
She replied, "Sir, try the fiction section."

W. C. Fields said, "If at first you don't succeed, try again and again. Then try again. Then give up! No sense in being a damned fool."

Dr. Powers told us once: "Time changes everything, even in Chicago. On one occasion when I was speaking in Chicago, I pointed out that Chicago used to be the stockyard of the nation and perhaps even the world. Yet a few weeks ago when I was walking down the street, a woman came up to me, pointed to my leather jacket and said, 'A cow had to die for that leather jacket.'"

Dr Powers replied, "I didn't know there were any witnesses, so apparently we're going to have to kill you too."

ৢৢৢ

Talking about Chicago and how things change reminded me about the time one of my friends went to the windy city on a business trip. Peter was a little concerned about driving in Chicago, but he needed a car to get to his many appointments. Rumor had it that the Chicago cops could be rather rough. One of his more experienced acquaintances told him, "Don't sweat it. Put a five-dollar bill inside your driver's licence." (Thirty-five years ago, $5 was the equivalent of $50 today.)

His friend continued. "If you are stopped, you hand your licence to the cop. He'll take the $5 and give you a warning."

Well, Peter took his friend's advice, and sure enough he was stopped for an illegal turn. The cop asked for Peter's licence, and Peter dutifully handed it to him. When he found the $5 he asked, "What's this?"

Peter mumbled something about always keeping an extra $5 in his licence. *Sure Peter, a Canadian with a U.S. $5 bill in his licence?*

As sales requested it. As marketing ordered it.

As manufacturing built it. As supply delivered it.

As plant installed it. As advertising sold it.

What the customer wanted.

The cop said, "Well, young man, I was going to give you a warning, but now you get a ticket!"

ʊʊʊ

Now how about a wee bit of Irish humor? I like it. My ancestors were Irish.

At a wake for Paddy, some of his friends were reminiscing: "Remember when Paddy got a ticket for speeding? The cop came up with his ticket book open, and Paddy said, "Right, I'll have a coke and a burger to go."

ʊʊʊ

Even when we Irish are joking, we're serious.

On another occasion, a patrolman was on the edge of town stopping speeders. Paddy was going about sixty-five miles an hour, and that's above the speed limit. The cop turned on his red and blue lights and the siren and took off after Paddy. Paddy accelerated to ninety-two miles an hour before the patrolman was able to stop him.

The cop snarled, "You crazy man? Didn't you see the flashing lights and hear the siren?"

"I sure did," replied Paddy.

"Well, why didn't you stop?", the irate cop queried.

Paddy answered him, "About three months ago, a highway patrolman stopped my wife, and she ran off with him. I thought you might be bringing her back."

ʊʊʊ

On St. Patrick's day, a few years ago, three Irishmen decided to celebrate this holy day in the holiest way possible by taking a tour of the local brewery. Three went, but only two came back. These two stalwarts went up and knocked on Mrs. Kelly's door. When she answered, one of them said, "Good afternoon to you, Mrs. Kelly."

She replied, "Good afternoon, where is Daniel? Is he dawdling again?"

The fellows say, "You know, Mrs. Kelly, in honor of St. Paddy's day, the three of us took a tour of the brewery."

"Yes, yes I'm aware of that," she replied.

"Well the highlight of the tour was this vat of beer. It wasn't just a vat of beer. It was a VAT of beer. We walked up about five stories until we were looking at an ocean of beer. Can you imagine a more beautiful vision, Mrs. Kelly?"

She says, "I suppose it was quite impressive, but what about Daniel?"

"Well, you know, Danny wanted to get a better look, you see, so he walked to the very edge. He leaned in a bit too far, and he fell in and drowned."

Mrs. Kelly exclaimed, "Oh my Lord, the poor man never had a chance."

"Well, Mrs. Kelly," one of the fellows admitted, "he actually did! He got out three times to go to the bathroom."

❦❦❦

A Texan walked into a pub in Ireland and cleared his voice to speak to this crowd of drinkers. He said, "I hear you Irish are a bunch of drinking fools. I'll give $500 American to anybody in here who can drink ten pints of Guinness back to back."

The room fell quiet and no one took the Texan up on the offer. One man even left the bar. But thirty minutes later, the one who left was back. He tapped the Texan on the shoulder and asked, "Is your bet still good?"

The Texan replied, "It sure is little buddy."

The bartender lined up the ten pints of Guinness, and the little Irish man tore into all ten pints and drank them back-to-back. The other pub patrons cheered as the Texan looked on in amazement.

As he handed the Irishman his $500, he said, "If you don't mind me asking, where did you disappear to for thirty minutes?"

"No problem," the Irishman replied, "I went down the street to another pub first to see if I could do it."

❦❦❦

Hey, Lyle! If you're Irish, quit picking on the Irish. Okay! Let me tell you about Victor Kiam:

Victor K. Kiam II ("I liked the razor so much I bought the company") said, "I consider a consultant to be like a castrated bull."

❦❦❦

My neighbor saw it from a different point of view. He had this big old tomcat that used to go out every night terrorizing the neighborhood. When a large number of kittens with markings similar to 'tom's' started appearing, the neighbors started to complain. So my neighbor had old tom fixed.

"What happened afterwards?", I asked. "Does he still go out at night?"

"Oh sure," my neighbor replied, "But now he goes strictly as a consultant."

When Victor K. Kiam II worked at Playtex, bra sizes were classified as A, B, C, and D. Most of the men buying for their wives could not relate to that. So they changed the descriptions to 'ping pong,' 'ding dong,' and 'King Kong,' and 'holy cow.'

What does a training bra train?

Grace and Helen, friends of Victor's, loved to go on daily walks and chat away while doing so. Helen just loved to use acronyms whenever she could.

One day she said, "T.G.G.I.F."

Grace replied, "S.H.I.T."

Helen exclaimed, "Grace, you startle me. What you said!"

Grace commented, "Well, you said 'T.G.G.I.F.'"

Helen, "Sure, that means 'Thank Goodness Grace. It's Friday.'"

Grace replied, "Sorry, Helen. It's Thursday."

🐞🐞🐞

Commissioned salespeople are constantly prospecting for new leads. That fact can lead to some irreverent humor. For example:

A salesman went to confession. He said, "Forgive me, Father, for I have sinned."

"Who with, my son?"

"Well, I can't say, Father."

"Was it with Mrs. O'Leary from across the street?"

"Sorry, Father."

"Was it Kathy at Joe's Bar and Grill?"

"Can't say, Father."

"Was it with Widow Hurley over on Fifth Street?"

"Father, that's it."

Afterwards, a friend queried, "How did it go?"

"Well, my sins were not forgiven, but I picked up three new prospects."

☙☙☙

One time, a speaker was introduced as one of the smartest men in the business. When he rose to speak, he humbly stated that he was definitely not the smartest. He declared, "It's true. I only needed three terms in college to graduate—Eisenhower's, Kennedy's, and Johnson's."

When this speaker started his talk, he said, "Before I begin I need to know, are there any questions on anything I've said so far? Now listen up. I've got nothing to say, and I'm only going to say it once."

My inferiority complex is just as good as yours!

More irreverence!

When one pope died, he was met at the pearly gates, and St. Peter graciously showed him around. He noticed that the residences for popes were all rather modest, but a lawyer had a huge mansion overlooking the ocean. This pope asked, "Why?"

"Oh," St. Peter replied, "We have 250 popes up here, but that's the first lawyer ever."

☙☙☙

Another lawyer also made it to heaven, and everyone showed up to a gala festival—a great party in his honor. The lawyer was suitably impressed but stated that he could not understand.

"I shouldn't even be here, I'm only 55."

"Well, let's see. According to this, you are the oldest person we have ever admitted."

"But that can't be. I'm only 55 years old."

"We have the best computer system possible. It never makes a mistake. It cannot make a mistake. According to the hours billed while on earth, you are 106 years old."

☙☙☙

A more-worldly lawyer, on a visit to Las Vegas found his way to a famous house of local pleasure. He met the madam and made some inquiries.

"Do the ladies ever contract social diseases?"

"Oh rarely. We are very careful here, and it seldom happens."

"Do any of the girls ever get pregnant?"

"Oh yeah, sometimes."

"Do they ever carry their babies full term?"

"Of course, where do you think we get our lawyers?"

☙☙☙

On their way to a justice of the peace, a young couple was in a fatal car accident. While waiting outside the pearly gates for St. Peter, they wondered if they might still be married—in heaven. When St. Peter got to them, they asked him about it.

St. Peter replied, "I don't know. This is the first time anyone has asked that. Let me check it out."

After a couple of months, the young couple began to wonder if they really should get married in heaven, considering the eternal aspect of it. They wondered: "What if it doesn't work out? Are we stuck together forever?"

Finally, St. Peter returns with the good news, "Yes, you can be married in heaven."

"Great," says the couple. "But what if things don't work out? Could we get a divorce in heaven?"

With this, St. Peter showed a little exasperation, and he slammed his clipboard down.

"What's wrong?" exclaimed the frightened couple.

"Come on," says St. Peter. "It took me three months to find a priest up here. Can you imagine how long it would take to find a lawyer?"

☙☙☙

My friend Larry Hurd is a lawyer. He does lots of wills. One person asked him, "If I die intestate will the government get all my assets?"

Larry replied, "No, but the lawyers may get most of it."

☙☙☙

One of the stories Larry enjoys is about the reading of a will after an elderly gent expired. Larry admits that wills are not usually read in this formal fashion anymore. However, for the benefit of this story, the entire family was gathered in great anticipation for the reading of the will. During his lifetime, this old boy had amassed a large fortune. Thus, those who might benefit waited breathlessly to learn if they were included in his largesse. With a proper degree of ceremony, the lawyer opened the yellowed pages of the epistle and read, "Being of sound mind, I spent it all."

❧❧❧

Have you made your will? A middle-aged man came to see Larry, who inquired about the man's wife. "Perhaps she should be present also."

The old fellow chuckled, "I don't want her involved."

"Why is that?", Larry asked.

"Well, my three previous wives were all early birds. It seems to me that I was the worm." "Also," the client stated, "I wouldn't say, now, that my current wife always gets her way, but she is the only person I know who writes her diary ten days in advance."

What is brown and black and looks good on a lawyer? A Doberman Pincer!

Humor abounds in the courts. Lawyers and witnesses are both guilty of gaffs and slips of the tongue. The following examples were taken from court reporter Mary Louise Gilman's book, *Humor in the Court*. Now don't laugh unless you mean it. You are under oath here:

"Did you ever stay all night with this man in New York?"
"I refuse to answer that question."
"Did you ever stay all night with this man in Chicago?"
"I refuse to answer that question."
"Did you ever stay all night with this man in Miami?"
"No. Oops!"

❧❧❧

Some of these lawyers are not exactly Perry Mason, as you can tell from the following questions:

"Doctor, how many autopsies have you performed on dead people?"
   "All of my autopsies have been performed on dead people."

"Do you know how far pregnant you are right now?"
   "I will be three months on November 8th."
   "Apparently then the date of conception would be August 8th."
   "Yes."
   "What were you and your husband doing at that time?"

"Were you acquainted with the defendant?"
   "Yes sir."
   "Before or after he died?"

"Mrs. Jones, do you believe you are emotionally unstable?"
   "I should be."
   "How many times have you committed suicide?"
   "Four times."
   Mrs. Jones, is your appearance here today pursuant to a disposition notice that I sent to your lawyer?"
   "No, this is how I dress when I go to work."

"When he went, had you gone and had she, if she wanted to and were able, for the time being excluding all the restraints on her not to go, gone also, would he have brought you, meaning you and she, with him to the station?"
   "Objection!" from the opposing lawyer. "That question should be taken out and shot."

Talk is cheap, if lawyers don't do the talking!

These days, it seems that we are bombarded with surveys. Companies are trying to find out what we think of their products. Sometimes, they even pay for the privilege of getting you to answer a few questions. One company offered me $25 if I would agree to their ten-minute survey. I told them, "Sure, I don't know anything about your product, but I want your $25." I got it too!

❦❦❦

Guilty! Now what's the charge?

One survey company knew they were in trouble when written replies to their questions started coming back with strange answers. One, for example:

Age: Nuclear
Birth: Caesarian section
Church preference: A colonial brick house
Sex: Once in Atlanta

❦❦❦

Did you hear about the dumb dog that was stealing and hiding ice cubes? His owners could not believe how dumb he was until they discovered that he had already hidden a bottle of scotch. (If you think that story is a bit dumb, how come you chuckled when you read it?)

❦❦❦

One day, a highly successful business owner discovered a college buddy sitting on a park bench looking like a derelict. A few discreet inquiries confirmed that his friend was, in fact, destitute. He said to the guy, "You know I think I can help you out. My porch needs painting, and the paint is right there with all the brushes and paint thinners. I'll pay you $500 to paint it for me. It will probably need two coats."

Some time later, his down-and-out friend showed up to collect his pay.

"Done already?"

"Yep, it only needed one coat. And by the way, it's not a Porsche, it's a Ferrari."

❦❦❦

"Boy, this food is fit for a king. Here King, here King." (You're right, it's corny and I can't resist it.)

❦❦❦

Four priests were playing golf. Father Murphy was 6 foot 4 inches and weighed 250 pounds. He died of a heart attack on the ninth hole, located furthest from the clubhouse. When they got him to the pro shop, the attendant was mightily impressed. He asked, "My gosh, how did you ever carry him all that distance?"

One of the three replied, "Oh that wasn't such a great problem, but putting him down and picking him up between shots was sure tough."

❧❧❧

One Sunday, a minister left his assistant to conduct services, while he went to play golf. To avoid running into any of his parishioners, he drove to a golf course in another town, and he played by himself. St. Peter noticed this, and pointed it out to God. "You're not going to let him get away with it, are you?"

God shook his head.

On his first shot, the minister had an awesome drive to score a hole in one nearly 280 yards away.

St. Peter scowled, "I thought you were going to punish him? You let him get a hole in one."

God chuckled, "Who is he going to tell?"

Success is getting what you want; happiness is wanting what you get!

A parishioner went to confession. "Father I have sinned. I stole a truckload of lumber."

The priest scolded him and said, "My son, for penance you must make a novena."

The sinner replied, "Father, I don't know how to make a novena, but if you have the plans, I've got the lumber."

Young woman's lament: The world is full of good men until you meet them!

Abe Lincoln, when running for the presidency, was accused by an irate woman of having two faces. He replied: "Madam, if I had two faces, why in the world would I be wearing this one?"

❧❧❧

One day, the bartender noticed a man at the end of the bar who looked very glum. The bartender asked, "What's wrong?"

The guy replied, "I've got an I.Q. of 187, and I can't find anyone to talk with. It's very depressing."

Another patron overheard him and stated, "Hey there, I've got an I.Q. of 190. I would love to have a conversation with someone like you." So they began talking about various theories of time, space, velocity, mass, and all that stuff. You know, like, "If I drive my car at the speed of light, what happens to the beam from the head lights?"

At the other end of the table, there was another guy looking pretty sad, and he stated that he could not find anyone to talk with. His problem was that he had an I.Q. of 60. Another guy overheard this and almost shouted, "Hey, I've got an I.Q. of 57. Let's talk."

He came over and sat down at once.

"Okay," said the first, "Tell me, do you prefer to sell term or whole life?"

Spouses are like regular customers.
If you don't tell them how much you appreciate them,
they will take their business elsewhere.

One night in bed, the husband grew somewhat amorous, only to be rebuffed by his wife. "Not tonight dear—I'm not in the mood."

"Is that your final answer?", he asked.

"Yes."

"Then, I think I'll call a friend," he replied.

❦❦❦

On another occasion on "Who Wants to be a Millionaire," a contestant used up all of his lifelines on the first question. The question was: "Who is your father?"

❦❦❦

One morning, a doctor and his wife got into a terrible argument. As the doctor left for his office, he made one parting comment, "Furthermore, you're lousy in bed."

With that cruel remark, he slammed the door and left. Later, he was feeling like a toad for having been so rude to his wife. He decided to telephone her and make amends. The phone rang and rang. Finally, his wife answered, somewhat out of breath.

His first remark was: "Where were you?"

"In bed," she replied.

"In bed? What were you doing in bed?", he queried.

"Getting a second opinion," she replied, demurely.

☙☙☙

An acquaintance admitted to me one day that he had struck his wife on one occasion. I was shocked. "Come off it, Joe. You would never strike your wife."

"I did," he confirmed.

"Why would you strike her? I can't believe it."

"She told me I was a lousy lover."

"For that you struck her?"

"No, no. I hit her for knowing the difference."

☙☙☙

Let me tell you about a salesman who must have been motivated! This is the story about Goering and Hitler in the days when the Third Reich was coming to power and Hitler was telling Goering to frame legislation, that would rob the Jewish people without bloodshed.

Goering said, "No, we can't do that, the Jews are smart, and any laws that we make up they will get around."

Hitler replied, "Nonsense, they are not smarter than our people!"

Goering smirked, "All right, put on your hat, come with me, and I will show you."

So they went down the street to a German shop and went in. Goering said to the shopkeeper, "I want some left-handed tea cups."

Now, the German shopkeeper said, "Left-handed tea cups, right-handed tea cups? There are no left-handed teacups! Left-handed tea cups and right-handed tea cups are all the same."

Then Goering took Hitler across the street to a shop run by a little Jewish shopkeeper. He said, "We want some left-handed tea cups."

The motivated Jewish salesman looked at them. "Are you lucky! If you had come in here yesterday and asked for left-handed teacups, I could not have helped you. But just this morning, this very morning, by mistake, *a pure mistake it was*, a large order of left-handed tea cups was delivered to me."

As they left the shop with the teacups, Goering said to Hitler, "There, see, I told you, they are much smarter than our people."

Hitler huffed, "They're not smarter. He was just lucky. You heard him say himself the left-handed tea cups were delivered by mistake."

🐛🐛🐛

It's an exciting feeling to know you have done a good job. For example:

A World War II navy dive-bomber pilot took off from an aircraft carrier with his squadron to bomb a Japanese ammunition dump. They ran into heavy resistance from anti-aircraft fire. All the other planes in his squadron were shot down, but he spotted the target and was able to dive in and make a direct hit. He ducked into the clouds and headed out to sea. He ran into heavy rain, and then it turned into a typhoon. He was having trouble controlling his plane, and then his entire instrument panel went out. He fought his way through the typhoon and fifteen minutes later came out on top of the clouds only to be attacked by seven Japanese Zero's.

With great skill, he shot down six of them and ran the other one off. Hopelessly lost, he was still on top of the clouds and almost out of fuel. When a hole opened in the clouds, he could see the carrier below him. He dived through the hole and made a perfect landing on the carrier just as he ran out of gas. He was so excited he threw back the canopy and shouted, "How did I do, guys?"

The crisp reply was, "You make just one mistake, Yankee!"

🐛🐛🐛

There were once two young identical twin boys. (I guess it's redundant to say two identical twins. I am reminded of a sign that says, "We must stamp out and abolish redundancy.") One of these little boys was a hopeless optimist and the other was an equally hopeless pessimist. Naturally, the parents took them to a child psychologist.

The learned doctor stroked his beard and said, "Do you want to level them off? On their next birthday, give the little pessimist the best toys you can afford. In a separate room, give the little optimist a box of manure for his present. That will level them off."

So the parents did this, and after distribution of the gifts, they peeked into the room where the little pessimist was looking at these beautiful toys and talking to himself. They heard, "I don't' like the color of that. I bet this will break. I know another kid who's got a better toy car than this"—same old dirge of pessimism.

So the parents tiptoed across the corridor and peeked in. They saw that their little optimist was throwing the manure up in the air and saying. "You can't fool me. Where there's this much manure, there's got to be a pony somewhere!"

One speaker related that anecdote to his audience, and afterwards one young lady came up and asked, "So where was the pony actually?"

❦❦❦

If you will permit a slight departure from humor, that story of those twin boys somehow illustrates for me the very principle that either releases a person into a full, enjoyable, and happy life or constricts, stifles, and diminishes our joyful participation in life. It's this. Each of us sees reality in a unique way. We each have a unique vision of reality— a unique expectancy of life. When we look at reality with our minds, we each see something quite different. And it's this highly personalized vision that makes us alive, welcomes us to a full and happy life or paints us into a small, dark corner of life. It's this vision—this way of perceiving reality, that matters.

You may remember the rhyming couplet: "Two men looked out from prison bars; one saw mud and one saw stars." Or that other verse:

> As you ramble through life,
> My brother, my sister, whatever be your goal,
> Keep your eye upon the donut and not upon the hole.

What a tragedy it would be to die without having really lived; to let all these beautiful days of life sift through the sands of the hourglass without ever savoring them. Why do so many people lead partial lives instead of full lives? There are so many people who fool everybody by breathing.

Take, for instance, the fifth grade teacher who received an anonymous note from one of the brats that he was teaching. It read, "If you feel all right, would you notify your face?"

❦❦❦

The following little exaggeration illustrates the point that we take our perceived situation too seriously at times and fail to perceive reality. This is an example from Dr. Mack Douglas:

There was a chap who constantly repeated, "I'm a dead man."

His friends chided him; "You're not dead. We can see you and hear you. Don't be ridiculous; you are not dead."

Nothing they could say mattered. In spite of their efforts, he continued to repeat, *ad nauseam*, "I'm a dead man."

In exasperation, they took him to a psychiatrist. After an intensive investigative examination, the doctor advised his client as follows: "For two weeks, I want you to refrain from saying 'I'm a dead man.' Instead, I want you to say, 'Dead men don't bleed.'"

For the next two weeks, the patient dutifully repeated, as instructed, "Dead men don't bleed." This was almost as irritating to his friends as the original obsession, but they were able to tolerate it for two weeks to help their friend. At the end of the period, the patient returned to the doctor, who re-examined him. Did you say, "Dead men don't bleed" instead of "I'm a dead man?"

"Yes, doctor, I did."

"Let me hear you say it."

"Dead men don't bleed. Dead men don't bleed."

The doctor then took out an instrument and pricked the end of a finger. Blood gushed forth. The patient stared at it in horror. Suddenly, he exclaimed, "Oh, my god, dead men *do* bleed."

How often, in real life, do we hold onto our views and beliefs, ridiculous as they may be, in spite of evidence to the contrary? When faced with the choice of changing our views or providing proof of the value of our views, most people get busy on the proof.

❦❦❦

Bob Edwards was famous, or notorious, depending on your view point, as editor of the *Eye Opener*. He stated, "To do right is easy when sin is no longer a pleasure." He also said, "Forgive your enemies today! If you have no enemies forgive some of your friends today!"

❦❦❦

Stuart Smith of Birmingham, England, joined the Royal Navy at age fifteen. He had a choice—join Her Majesty's forces or be sent to a farm in South Wales. Since he didn't fancy being part of any cheap labor scheme, he decided on the navy. Sometime after his indoctrination, he was sent with the fleet to La Spazia, in Northern Italy. It was an extra-special occasion, as the British fleet had not visited Italy since the war. The admiral on his ship was trying to get the pilot boat to come along the port side. Out of desperation, he transmitted over the ship's intercom, "Any personnel speaking Italian report to the bridge immediately."

On hearing this, for a bit of a laugh, Stuart smartly left the ranks of the men lined up around the side of the ship and rushed to the bridge. He approached the admiral and saluted formally. The admiral asked brusquely, "Do you speak Italian, Smith?"

"Yes, sir."

The admiral handed Stuart the megaphone and commanded, "Ask that Italian pilot boat to come along side the port side."

Stuart saluted crisply and replied, "Hey-A, sir." He accepted the megaphone and shouted, "Hey manio in the boatio, come along the port sideio."

The last thing he heard as he swiftly disappeared down the hatch and back to the flight deck was, "Put that man on detention."

That bit of irreverence got him fouteen days punishment.

"But," says Stuart; "it was worth it."

There before him was the whole ship's company curled up in hysterics.

Goethe said:
"Whatever you can do, or dream you can, begin it.
Boldness has genius, power, and magic in it!"

If something is said or written by someone famous often enough, (maybe once is enough) we tend to give that person credit for it. It may not be his or hers at all. Nevertheless, we start quoting them, and it becomes theirs by default. They may never have claimed it. They just use it and, if no one else claims it, it's theirs. An example: Harvey Mackay says, "I have a favorite aphorism: *'A goal is a dream with a deadline.'*"

The only part of that saying that I have never heard before is "I have a favorite aphorism." The rest of the line I have heard many times from many sources. However, I do not know who said it first. So let's give it to Harvey.

There is humor to be found in arrogance:

Donald Connelly of Boston tells a story about a very successful surgeon who bought a Mercedes. He took it in for service. While he was waiting, a loud-mouthed mechanic said: "Hey, Mr. Fancy Doctor come over here. Doc, you and I do the same thing. We work on hearts. See this car? See these valves? That's the heart of this engine. When these valves are broken, I take them out and fix them. I polish them up and put them back. When I'm done, this thing purrs like a kitten. You and I do the same thing, Doc. How come you get the big bucks?"

The surgeon leaned over, peered at the valves, and said, "Try doing it with the engine running."

❦❦❦

Benjamin Zander, conductor of the Boston Philharmonic, has a great story about Toscanini:

There are many stories about conductors, most of them told by orchestra players. One of my favorites is the one about Toscanini, who was a very great conductor and a great galvanizer of people, but he had a legendary temper. In the middle of a rehearsal, he shouted at one of the double bass players who had exasperated him, "You're fired!" (This was in the days before the union.) This poor man had to go home and tell his wife he didn't have a job.

As he was leaving the room for the last time, he turned and said to Toscanini, "You're a no-good son-of-a-bitch!"

Toscanini shouted back, "It's too late to apologize."

❦❦❦

When Arthur Fiedler, famous conductor of the Boston Pops Orchestra, came to Calgary, on one occasion, he displayed his great sense of humor. Our "pops" event was held in The Corral, an old hockey arena. The audience was seated on the main level where ice would normally be. A stage was erected at one end for the orchestra and it's conductor. A group from the local Jaycees was recruited to serve wine and champagne to the paying patrons. Our reward and the incentive for serving was that we could meet the orchestra and it's famous conductor after the event. The evening started well enough. The audience was in high spirits, and the orchestra sounded magnificent.

About the time it launched into a touching rendition of "Clare de Lune," a hauntingly beautiful quiet piece, we started opening the champagne. Without thinking, we popped the corks, letting them fly twenty or more feet into the air. The audience thought it was funny. Each time a bottle opened, there was a distinct "pop." The audience tittered as the corks flew. Toward the end of that incredibly beautiful music, we realized that we were in trouble. This famous orchestra leader had every right to be furious with us. When the music concluded, Fiedler turned to the audience with a bow. For a poignant moment, he stood looking out at us. Everyone froze in anticipation of what was to come. Diminutive in stature he may have been, but he proved to be a giant in human relations. From his stern demeanor, he allowed a smile to spread across his face as he said, "Well, it is a 'pops' concert after all."

The audience roared its approval and honored him with thunderous applause. Nevertheless, from that point on, champagne corks were noticeably quiet.

❦❦❦

Many years ago, when Enrico Caruso was at the height of his career, there was a little group called "critics." Once when they got together after a performance, one young man said, "I know why he does so well. He has the best advance publicity in the history of show business."

Another one said, "Yes, and he plays the best theaters."

A third one added, "Yes, 100 violins. Never before in history has anyone had that kind of accompaniment."

Finally, an elderly critic sitting there said, "You know, I've listened to everything that has been said, and it's all true. But let me remind you that there comes a time in the evening when *Caruso must sing*."

Doesn't that happen to everyone? Sooner or later, we have to get out of the locker room and play the game.

❧❧❧

In our business society today, many companies employ efficiency experts. Here is an example of what may happen when such a specialist gets an opportunity to show his stuff:

An entrepreneur had tickets for an event with the New York Philharmonic for one of his favorites, Schubert's "Unfinished Symphony." Just prior to the evening, he was called out of town on business, so he could not use the tickets. He gave them to one of his key employees, an efficiency expert, or what is known as a "work-study management executive."

When the business owner got back to town, he wanted to know how the evening went. The work-study management executive was ready, and he handed his boss a written report. It went something like this:

A: For considerable time, the oboe players had nothing to do. Their number should be reduced and their work should be spread over the whole orchestra, thus eliminating peaks of activity.

B: All the violins are playing identical notes. This seems like an unnecessary duplication. The staff in this section should be drastically cut. If the large volume of sound is really required, it could be obtained by the use of an electronic amplifier.

C: Much effort was absorbed in the playing of semi-quavers. This seems an excessive refinement, and it's recommended that all notes be rounded off to the nearest eight note. If this were done, it would be possible to use trainees and lower-grade operators.

D: No useful purpose is served by repeating with the horns the passage that has already been handled by the strings. If such redundant passages had been eliminated, the concert could have been reduced from two hours to twenty minutes. If Schubert had only paid attention to these details, he probably would have been able to finish his symphony after all.

This story reminded me of an anecdote my friend John King likes to tell. One of his favorite pieces of music is Beethoven's "Ninth Symphony." In the middle section of this symphony, there is a significant period when the string bass section had nothing to do. Rather than sit idly by, these players would often leave the orchestra pit until they were required again.

On one such occasion, one of the players suggested that the group should go across the street to the pub. Well, during their imbibing and in their enjoyment of these stolen moments, they lost track of time.

Suddenly one player exclaimed, "Oh my gosh, we had better get back or we will be late."

Another member of the string bass section laughingly replied, "Don't worry. We have time yet, because I tied together the conductor's pages to the last score. It will take a while for him to get them untied."

When they got back, the conductor was furious. It was the bottom of the ninth, the basses were loaded, and the score was tied.

❦❦❦

Did you hear about the frog that consulted a psychic? The psychic advised the frog, "You will meet a beautiful young lady who will want to know everything about you."

"Where, when?", the frog asked excitedly.

"Next year in biology class," replied the psychic.

Is the following story just a matter of confidence or was there a hint of arrogance?

In 1927, the New York Yankees were about to play the Pittsburgh Pirates in the World Series. A reporter asked Babe Ruth, "Are you concerned about the Pittsburgh Pirates?"

Ruth replied, "No. Should I be concerned about them?"

The reporter answered, "Well, they have six great starting pitchers."

Ruth exclaimed, "Really? What good are six great starting pitchers going to do for you in a four-game series?"

Babe Ruth averaged 400 and hit two home runs. The Yankees swept the Pirates in four games.

Arrogance or simple truth?

Pablo Picasso was sitting at a sidewalk café in Paris. An American tourist approached him, interrupted Picasso's lunch, and asked him for a sketch. Good-naturedly, Picasso reached for a napkin, drew a sketch, and gave it to the guy.

Somewhat shocked, the tourist said, "Mr. Picasso, I want to pay you for this sketch."

"No, you probably don't want to pay me for this sketch," Picasso replied.

"But I insist on paying you," stated the American.

"All right;" Picasso replied, "that will be $10,000."

The American tourist was taken aback. "Mr. Picasso, it took you only ten seconds to draw that sketch."

Picasso replied, "Yes, it did, but it took me a lifetime to reach those ten seconds."

Humor can come from an irrational source:

A little elderly lady approached a seminar leader after he had finished his talk on estate planning. She was a diminutive grandmotherly type— about five feet tall. She proceeded to tell the speaker that her husband had passed away over two years before, and she was still involved in settling the estate. The bulk of his assets were with a mutual fund company. She asked, "Can you help me?"

The speaker replied, "No, it's in the hands of the lawyers."

The little lady looked him right in the eye and said, "This is so frustrating. I almost wish he hadn't died."

In some situations, there is not much difference between arrogance and ignorance:

One day, a guy drove off a road, and his car was stuck in a ditch. A farmer saw him, and the guy said, "Could you help me? I see you're plowing your field with a mule."

The farmer said, "Yeah, that's my mule Buddy. I'll bring Buddy down there. He'll pull your car right up out of the ditch."

The driver allowed, "Well, I'd be very appreciative of that."

And so Buddy got hooked up to the car, and the farmer hit Buddy once on the rear and said, "Pull, Jumbo."

Buddy didn't even move.

The farmer hit him again and said, "Pull, Henry."

Nothing!

Then he hit the mule on the rear again and said, "Pull, Buddy."

Buddy pulled the car right up out of the ditch. No problem!

The errant driver, just about to drive away, gave the farmer a few bucks for his effort and then he asked the farmer, "Look, I've got to ask you something. Why did you hit your mule twice and call him by the wrong name?"

The farmer replied, "Well, it's simple. My mule Buddy is blind, and if he thought he was pulling your car up out of the ditch all alone, he never would have done it."

Team work!

The trouble with the economy today is that, if a person is rich, it's always on paper. If you're broke, however, it's always in cash!

A financial planning salesman, deciding to improve his sales skills, attended a twelve-week seminar. In the twelfth week, the class had a speaking contest. It was called the "Sales Talk Championship." The financial planning salesman won. He was awarded a plaque, which read, "Sales Talk Champion." When he received his reward, he blurted out, "Oh golly, where can I hang it. Obviously not in my office. Can you imagine Tom and Nancy coming in and reading it?"

Nancy might say, "Oh look Tom, this plaque says, 'Sales Talk Champion'."

Tom would probably reply, "Right, and you think we should give him all our money?"

There is only one letter different between save and have. To have it, however, you must save it!

A client of a financial planner came to his office to discuss a tax shelter that had turned sour. When he asked for the financial planner, the office manager informed the client that the financial planner had died. Upon hearing this, the client turned around and walked out. Three days later, the same ex-client was back, and again he asked for the financial planner. Once again, the office manager explained that the financial planner had died. The ex-client, as before, turned around and walked out.

The following week, he was back for the third time. By now, the office manager was somewhat piqued. He exclaimed, "Look, I told you the financial planner you are asking for died. Why do you keep coming back?"

The ex-client smiled, "Yes, but I like the way it sounds."

A long-term financial decision for some geriatrics is deciding to buy green bananas at the supermarket.

A salesman in Chicago was greatly distressed because his flight had been canceled. There was a long line-up while people were waiting to be re-booked. The overbearing salesman charged to the front of the line and said, "I have to get out of here. I have to get out of here."

The gate agent was trying to smile and work as efficiently as she could. The salesman insisted on how important he was. "Do you know who I am, lady?"

Calmly she picked up the microphone and announced, "Attention, attention, does anyone in the room know who this gentleman is? He seems to have lost his identity."

The salesman became belligerent.

Patiently, she explained, "Sir, you will have to wait in line like everyone else."

Arrogantly, he exclaimed, "Screw you, lady."

Without taking her eyes off the computer terminal, she replied, "Yeah, well you will have to get in line for that too."

❦❦❦

Many of us travel a lot on business. It would be hard to do a full year without ever losing your luggage, at least for a few hours. That's why we try to carry it on board whenever possible. One salesman learned the lesson on laughter quite well. On his next trip after his luggage had been sent halfway around the world, he approached the airline counter with a big smile on his face. If you can't do anything about the situation, what do you do? Laugh!

He was on his way to Boston. He said to the lady at the counter, "I would like you to send this bag to Detroit and this one to Miami."

She replied, "I'm sorry sir, we can't do that."

"You can't?", he queried. "You did it last time I flew."

❧❧❧

Another salesman, used to be a frequent flyer with Continental Airlines. They had a bad reputation for losing bags. Jim quipped, "I fooled them on this trip. I checked my bags straight through to lost and found."

In the morning newspaper, Jim noticed an article that claimed Continental had lost $2 million in the last quarter. Jim told his audience about the article and quipped, "They probably put it in one of my suitcases."

❧❧❧

Loretta LaRoche has contributed the following humorous witticism about dirty underwear:

Mothers sometimes say, "Remember always wear clean underwear. You never know when you might be in an accident." Okay, but have you ever seen a sign left by a paramedic on a body that read, "We couldn't take it—the underwear was dirty."

❧❧❧

Loretta says: "Eccentrics live longer. Move out of your bedroom backwards once in a while. Tell yourself, I don't know whether I'm coming or going."

Loretta suggests that when you are traveling by plane and you have to go through the first-class section say: "Peasant coming through!"

Loretta's humorous view of the differences between men and women can be summed up as follows: "Hunters take themselves too seriously. Women laugh at themselves more readily. That's why they take so long in the ladies' room. They are in there cracking up."

"Women ask for directions. Men don't. That's why Moses was in the desert for forty years. If Moses had a woman with him, she would have asked the burning bush."

Loretta offers a thumbnail philosophy of life: "If you think the worst and get the worst, you suffer twice. If you think the best and get the worst, you only suffer once."

If someone tells you, "You're too much," just reply, "You're damned right, and I'm going to be even more."

She says about her childhood, "We laughed every stinking day, because life's amusing. Life is very, very funny. And everyone is a joke. We are all a joke, but no one gets it."

My wife claims that I'm always getting lost and that I won't ask for directions. She just doesn't appreciate that I'm investigating alternate routes.

Even though I grew up on a farm in the east, I never could understand the ways of farmers. One day, my dad and I drove over to a neighbor to borrow a set of discs. Our set had plum worn out. Dad had ordered a new set, but they had not yet arrived. We found our neighboring farmer in his yard. The set of discs we were after sat there in plain view. My best friend Johnny was working in the field on the one and only tractor. The discs were not in use. There was only one question to be asked, "Can we borrow your discs?"

Well, they greeted, and they talked. They talked and they talked, as though time meant nothing. I was getting more and more agitated. There was about forty acres waiting for me to disc. The weather was perfect, and I wanted to get at it. But they talked about everything except the discs.

Thinking about that experience, I was reminded of the story about a salesman who had graduated from Georgia State with a master's degree in business. His expertise was in time control. Joe, the college grad, and another salesman started making sales calls together on potential estate planning clients.

One day, they drove out into the country to see a South Georgia farmer. They waited for three hours at the side of a fence watching the old farmer watering his hogs. First, the farmer would separate one hog from the herd, drive it to the branch, water him, and then drive it back. Then, he would get the next one. Finally, when he had finished with all of them, the time-control specialist said to the farmer, "If you drove all of them down to the branch at once, you would save a lot of time."

The old farmer looked at this young college graduate and replied; "Ah heck, time don't mean nothing to no hog."

❧❧❧

At my age, I'm often asked what I would do differently if I had it to do all over again. In answer to that, I like the following poem written by Nadine Stair (85 years old) of Louisville, Kentucky. This story may be more inspirational than humorous, and it probably has been published elsewhere. I have never seen it in any other publication. I got it from a speaker who claims he got it directly from the author:

> If I had my life to live over, I'd dare to make more mistakes next time. I'd relax. I'd limber up. I would be sillier than I have this time. I would take fewer things seriously. I would take more chances. I would take more trips. I would climb more mountains and swim more rivers. I would eat more ice cream and less beans. I would perhaps have more actual troubles, but I'd have fewer imaginary ones.
>
> You see, I am one of those people who live sensibly and sanely, hour after hour, day after day.
>
> Oh, I've had my moments, and if I had it to do over again, I'd have more of them. In fact, I'd try to have nothing else. Just moments, one after another, instead of living so many years ahead of each day. I've been one of these persons who never goes anywhere without a thermometer, a hot water bottle, a raincoat and a parachute. If I had it to do over again, I would travel lighter than I have. If I had my life to live over, I would start barefoot earlier in the spring and I would stay that way later in the fall. I would go to more dances. I would ride more merry-go-rounds. I would pick more daisies.

Now when someone in my presence is a little up-tight about something, I advise him or her, "You should pick more daisies."

❧❧❧

In any sales business, the message to new people is always the same. "See the people—tell the miracle—see the people. You'll do fine. Don't panic!" This sales training is almost like the written words of instruction designed for the United States Peace Corps for volunteers going to serve in the Amazon. These were the written instructions:

What to do if attacked by an anaconda, the largest snake in the world. It is related to the boa constrictor and can be as large as 35 feet long and weigh as much as 300–400 lbs.

If you are attacked by an anaconda, do not run. The snake is faster than you are. Lie flat on the ground. Put your hands tight against your sides—your legs tight against one another—pull your chin in. The snake will come and begin to nudge and climb all over your body—do not panic!

After the snake has examined you, it will begin to swallow you from the feet end—always from the feet end. Permit the snake to swallow your feet and ankles—do not panic. The snake will now begin to suck your legs into his body—you must lie perfectly still—this will take a long time. When the snake has reached your knees, slowly and with as little motion as possible reach down, take your knife and very gently slide it into the side of the snake's mouth, between the edge of its mouth and your leg, suddenly rip upwards, severing the snake's head.

The last two suggestions were the ones that got me. They were:

1. Be sure your knife is sharp.
2. Be sure you have your knife!

❧❧❧

Anyone who has ever been recruited for a sales position or a speaking gig can relate to this next story. All too often, the job sounds too good to be true. Only later do we discover the truth.

A young lady died and when she met St. Peter at the pearly gates she was given two choices, Heaven or Hell. Saint Peter said, "You must experience both before you can make a decision."

So this young speaker was sent off to Heaven for a week. She had never seen such beauty. There were babbling brooks, light breezes, beautiful flowers, and a banquet of good food. So after a week of heavenly experience, she returned to St. Peter and informed him that she did not really need to visit Hell. Her mind was made up—she wanted to go to Heaven.

St. Peter informed her that she must visit Hell, and she was promptly sent there. Well, Hell was not what this professional speaker expected. Hell was a gorgeous mahogany bar, with extremely handsome waiters serving an unlimited supply of exotic drinks. Of course, all of her speaking buddies were there, so she felt right at home. After a week of partying with her buddies, this young speaker informed St. Peter that she had made a mistake. Hell was where she wanted to be after all. St. Peter banished her to Hell for eternity. When she returned, the bar was deserted. There were cobwebs everywhere. There were no handsome waiters and no speaking buddies, but Satan was at the bar laughing.

This naïve professional speaker said, "Excuse me, but I was just here less than twenty-four hours ago and this place was 'jammin'. What happened?"

Satan gave his wry satanic smile and replied, "Yesterday, you were a recruit. *Today, you are the feature speaker.*"

❧❧❧

Fate sometimes does step in to affect our lives. We make decisions that allow things to happen to us. We take a different route to work and run into a speed trap. If we had left for our destination fifteen minutes earlier, we could have avoided the holdup caused by that accident. In retrospect, our decisions and our actions that follow seem somewhat ironic. Consider the fate of the young man from Baghdad:

There was once a merchant in the ancient city of Baghdad who sent his servant to the market to buy food.

Soon afterward, the servant returned, pale and trembling.

His voice stuttered as he said, "Master, just now when I was in the marketplace, I was touched by someone in the crowd and when I turned, I saw it was Death that touched me. Death looked at me and made a threatening gesture. Please, Master, let me have your horse and I will ride away from this city and avoid my fate. I will go to Samara and there, Death will not find me."

The merchant gave the servant his horse. The servant mounted it, dug his spurs into its flanks, and as fast as the horse could gallop, he went towards Samara.

Then the merchant went to the market, found Death, and asked. "Why did you make a threatening gesture to my servant when you saw him in the marketplace this morning?"

And Death answered, "That was not a threatening gesture. It was only a start of surprise. I was astonished to see him in Baghdad, for I had an appointment with him tonight in Samara."

❦❦❦

Perhaps some of you have heard of the man stranded on a high point of land as a major storm moved through the area. As the water began licking the threshold of his front door, a boat passed by and the pilot said, "Hop in, and I'll get you over to dry land."

The man replied, "Oh, no thanks; the Lord will take care of me." So the pilot moved on.

As the water continued to rise, the man climbed to the second floor, and, as he hung out of the window, another boat passed alongside and offered help. The man again replied, "Thanks much, but I'm trusting in my Lord to deliver me."

The flooding continued, and the man went out on the roof and was completely surrounded by water for as far as the eye could see. A helicopter came by and hovered overhead while the pilot offered assistance once more. Again the man responded, "I have faith in the Lord; He will deliver me."

So the helicopter moved on with its rescue mission. Subsequently, the man appeared at the gates of Heaven, and St. Peter asked of him, "What are you doing here?"

He replied, "I was waiting on the Lord and got drowned in a flood."

Saint Peter answered, "Oh, you're the guy. Well, we sent you two boats and a helicopter, what else were you waiting for?"

❦❦❦

There is another version of that story, supposedly a true story, which relates directly to the sales business. It also shows how one may put an old story to good use in answering a somewhat difficult objection to taking action, at some point in the sales procedure:

A life insurance saleslady met an obstinate prospect for a sales presentation. Try as she might, she could not get through to him. He answered all of her points with, "The Lord will provide."

Finally, she looked directly at him and asked, "Who do you think sent me to you?"

❧❧❧

One day, God was looking down at Earth and saw all of the evil that was going on. God decided to send an angel down to Earth to check it out. So God called on one of the best angels and sent the angel to Earth to do a study.

When the angel returned, the angel told God, "Yes, it is bad. On Earth, ninety-five percent are bad and only five percent are good.

God said, "This is not good."

So God decided to e-mail the five percent that were good. God wanted to encourage those who were good and give them a little something to help them keep going.

Do you know what the e-mail said?

You didn't get one either, huh?

How do you write '0' in Roman numerals?

Have you heard about the smoker who was feeling guilty about his habit? The more he read about smoking endangering his health, the worse he felt. So finally, he decided to give up reading.

❧❧❧

There is no such thing as a perfect husband, but the one in the following example is trying at least:

There are several men in the locker room of a private club after exercising. Suddenly, a cell phone that was on one of the benches rings. A man picks it up, and the following conversation ensues:

"Hello?"

"Honey, it's me. Are you at the club?"

"Yes."

"Great! I am at the mall two blocks from where you are. I saw a beautiful mink coat. It is absolutely gorgeous! Can I buy it?"

"What's the price?"

"Only $1,500."

"Well, okay, go ahead and get it if you like it that much."

"Ahhh, and I also stopped by the Mercedes dealership and saw the new models. I saw one I really liked. I spoke with the salesman, and he gave me a really good price, and since we need to exchange the BMW that we bought last year...?"

"What price did he quote you?"

"Only $75,000."

"Okay, but for that price, I want it with all the options."

"Great! Before we hang up, there is something else."

"What?"

"It might look like a lot, but I was reconciling your bank account, and I stopped by the real estate agent this morning, and I saw the house we had looked at last year. It's on sale! Remember? The one with a pool, English garden, acre of park area, beachfront property."

"How much are they asking?"

"Only $450,000, a magnificent price, and I see that we have that much in the bank to cover it."

"Well, then, go ahead and buy it, but just bid $420,000. Okay?"

"Okay, sweetie. Thanks! I'll see you later! I love you!"

"Bye. I do too." The man hung up, closed the phone's flap and raised his hand above his head and asked, "Does anyone know who this phone belongs to?"

✽✽✽

Another nearly perfect husband was visiting a friend's athletic club for the first time. They played a strenuous tennis match. Afterwards, while his friend went to talk to another member, Joey proceeded to the locker room, where he took off his soaking-wet tennis garb. He grabbed a towel off the rack and headed to the shower. While showering, he thought he heard female voices. He quickly completed his shower and toweled dry. By now, he could hear female voices clearly. He peered cautiously around the corner and, sure enough, there were several ladies between the shower room and his discarded clothes. He realized his mistake at once. He was in the ladies' locker room. There was no way of getting to his soggy clothes without being seen. His first reaction was to cover himself with the towel and just walk out.

But then he reasoned that he could be recognized and he would be embarrassed. Not only that, he considered the position of his host. To permit a guest to make such a *faux pas* would indeed be embarrassing. So he did the only logical thing. He covered his face with the towel leaving the rest of his body completely exposed. As he walked briskly through the ladies' locker room, past the assembled ladies, he heard one of them ask, "Who is that?"

One lady replied, "Well, it's not my husband."

Another lady commented, "Well, it's sure as hell not mine."

A third lady stated emphatically, "Hey, he's not even a member of the club."

❧❧❧

Here is some material contributed by Jeff Mowatt. Jeff wrote, "I thought you might enjoy this, passed on to me by a fellow speaker."

HOW TO IMPRESS A WOMAN

- Compliment her
- Cuddle her
- Kiss her
- Caress her
- Love her
- Stroke her
- Tease her
- Comfort her
- Protect her
- Hug her
- Hold her
- Spend money on her
- Wine and dine her
- Buy things for her
- Listen to her

- Care for her
- Stand by her
- Support her
- Go to the end of the earth for her

HOW TO IMPRESS A MAN

- Show up naked
- Bring beer

The following may be advice from a male chauvinist. You decide.

Ladies, this is what your man wants to say to you to begin the New Year:

- If you think you are fat, you probably are. Don't ask us. We refuse to answer.
- Learn to work the toilet seat. If it's up, put it down.
- If you won't dress like the Victoria's Secret girls, don't expect us to act like soap opera guys.
- Birthdays, Valentines, and anniversaries are not quests to see if we can find the perfect present yet again!
- If you ask a question you don't want an answer to, expect an answer you don't want to hear.
- Sometimes, we're not thinking about you. Live with it.
- Don't ask us what we're thinking about unless you are prepared to discuss such topics as beer choices, the shotgun formation, or monster trucks.
- Sunday = sports. It's like the full moon or the changing of the tides. Let it be.
- Shopping is not a sport, and, no, we're never going to think of it that way.
- When we have to go somewhere, absolutely anything you wear is fine.
- Really, you have enough clothes.
- Crying is blackmail. Ask for what you want.
- Let's be clear on this one: Subtle hints don't work. Strong hints don't work. Really obvious hints don't work. Just say it!
- NO, we don't know what day it is. We never will. Mark anniversaries on the calendar.

- Peeing standing up is more difficult. We're bound to miss sometimes.
- Most guys own three pairs of shoes. What makes you think we'd be any good at choosing which pair, out of thirty, would look good with your dress?
- 'Yes' and 'no' are perfectly acceptable answers to almost every question.
- Come to us with a problem only if you want help solving it. That's what we do. Sympathy is what your girlfriends are for.
- A headache that lasts for seventeen months is a problem. See a doctor.
- It is neither in your best interest nor ours to take the quiz together. No, it doesn't matter which quiz.
- Anything we said six months ago is inadmissible in an argument. All comments become null and void after seven days.
- If something we said could be interpreted two ways, and one of the ways makes you sad or angry, we meant the other one.
- Let us ogle. We're going to look anyway; it's genetic.
- You can either tell us to do something or tell us how to do something, but not both. Whenever possible, please say whatever you have to say during commercials.
- All men see in only sixteen colors. Peach is a fruit, not a color.
- If it itches, it will be scratched.
- If we ask what's wrong and you say "nothing," we will act like nothing's wrong. We know you're lying, but it's just not worth the hassle.
- What the heck is a doily?

❧❧❧

Here are some things you would never hear a redneck say, no matter how drunk he is, no matter how far from home he has wandered, and no matter how much the skunks are threatening:

- I'll take Shakespeare for 1000, Alex.
- Duct tape won't fix that.
- Honey, I think we should sell the pickup and buy a family sedan.

- Come to think of it, I'll have a Heineken.
- We don't keep firearms in this house.
- Has anybody seen the sideburns trimmer?
- You can't feed that to the dog.
- No kids in the back of the pickup; it's just not safe.
- Wrestling's fake.
- Honey, did you mail that donation to Greenpeace?
- We're vegetarians.
- Do you think my gut is too big?
- I'll have grapefruit and grapes instead of biscuits and gravy.
- Honey, we don't need another dog.
- Who gives a shit who won the Civil War?
- Give me the small bag of pork rinds.
- Too many deer heads detract from the décor.
- Spittin' is such a nasty habit.
- Trim the fat off that steak.
- The tires on that truck are too big.
- I've got it all on the C drive.
- Unsweetened tea tastes better.
- Would you like your fish poached or broiled?
- My fiancée, Bobbie Jo, is registered at Tiffany's.
- Checkmate.
- She's too young to be wearing a bikini.
- Does the salad bar have bean sprouts?
- Hey, here's an episode of "Hee Haw" that we haven't seen.
- Be sure to bring my salad dressing on the side.
- Those shorts ought to be a little longer, Darla.
- Nope, no more for me. I'm driving tonight.

❦❦❦

A male chauvinist redneck cowboy finally married his high school sweetheart. After the reception, this diehard determined that he should establish just who was boss in the family. On the very next morning, as they were dressing, the cowboy took his designer jeans and tossed them to his new bride.

She queried, "What do you want me to do with these?"

"Put them on; wear them," he replied.

"I can't wear these," she retorted. "They are much too big for me."

"Right," he snorted. "Just remember that. In our family, I wear the pants."

After a moment of reflection his lovely bride took off her panties and tossed them to her power-driven husband. "Here, let's see you wear these," she smirked.

"That's ridiculous," he chafed. "I can't get into these."

"Right," she snarled, "And you're never going to unless you change your attitude."

My brother Grant sent another contribution:

The Sunday before Christmas, a pastor told his congregation that the church needed some extra money. He asked the people to consider donating a little more than usual into the offering plate. He said that whoever gave the most would be able to pick out three hymns. After the offering plates were passed, the pastor glanced down and noticed that someone had placed a $1,000 bill in offering.

He was so excited that he immediately shared his joy with his congregation and said he'd like to personally thank the person who placed the money in the plate. A very quiet, elderly, saintly-looking lady all the way in the back shyly raised her hand. The pastor asked her to come to the front. Slowly, she made her way to the pastor. He told her how wonderful it was that she gave so much and, in thanks, asked her to pick out three hymns. Her eyes brightened as she looked over the congregation, pointed to the three most handsome men in the building and said, "I'll take him and him and him."

There is a little doggerel that goes like this:

> That money talks I'll not deny,
> I heard it once; it said *goodbye*!

Driving and drinking

In one Eastern Canadian province, driving while inebriated is still considered a sporting venture. One evening, while on a routine patrol, a policeman parked near a local tavern, as he had done many times before. Just after last call, the officer noticed a man stagger from the bar in such an intoxicated state that he could hardly walk. This patron stumbled around for a few minutes while the policeman quietly observed.

After what seemed like an eternity, while he tried his keys on five different vehicles, the obvious drunk managed to locate his own car. He opened the door and fell in. Leaning against the seat, he apparently dozed off for a few minutes while several other patrons left the bar and drove away.

Finally, the drunk roused himself and started his car. He switched the windshield wipers on and off several times, even though it was a clear dry night. He tested his horn, and then switched on the lights and tested the blinkers. He moved his car forward a few feet, then reversed a little. He sat still while several other vehicles left.

At last, he pulled out of the parking lot and started to drive away very slowly. The officer, who had waited patiently all this time, now started his car, turned on his flashing lights, and went after the slow-moving vehicle. He pulled the driver over and promptly administered a Breathalyzer test. To his amazement, the test showed no evidence that the man had consumed any alcohol whatever. Dumbfounded, the officer said, "I'll have to ask you to accompany me to the police station. This equipment must be faulty."

Oh, no, I doubt it," the chap stated clearly. "You see, tonight, I am the designated decoy."

❦❦❦

Some people are so well trained in looking at the details that they cannot see the big picture.

How the East sees the West!
"Designatied Driver"

How the West sees the East!

Czaba Sziklai, a clinical psychologist, talked to our sales group about his experience with sales people when they approach him to sell something. Most of us have had similar experiences.

How many of you here get unwanted, unsolicited telephone calls from somebody trying to sell you something? Do you notice that sometimes when you listen to those you can't help becoming cynical? You don't listen to what they are selling, but rather how they go about doing it. Do any of you get turned off by it? I take all those calls because I work with sales people and I'm interested. Of course, I'm at the point where I am beginning to wear a little thin. Let me give you a couple of examples:

This guy called and said: "Mr. Sziklai, my name is Mike, blah, blah, blah."

I knew then that I was not talking to a friend.

And he said, "How are you doing?"

And I said, "I'm doing great."

He said, "Oh, that's wonderful. That's great. Ah, that's fantastic."

After a while, he said, "Let me tell you what we're going to do for you."

And I said, "I can hardly wait."

"We're going to give you a week's free subscription to our newspaper."

And I said, "You know, Mike, I really appreciate this call, but I want you to know that I don't read newspapers, so I'm not interested."

He said, "Oh, that's great. That's very interesting, but let me tell you what else we're going to do. We are also going to give you a year's subscription at half price."

At that moment, I knew I was not connecting, so I said, "Let me tell you something that you probably didn't realize. I grew up in a Communist country. Every morning, we had to get up half an hour early to go to school and then at university read this two-page propaganda sheet and then get up and say some inane things about how great Communism is. Ever since, I've never touched a newspaper."

He said, "Oh, that is great. That is fantastic, wonderful." And he offered me another subscription. Well, you notice that there was something wrong with this picture. I was trying to tell him something, but he had learned not to listen. Salespeople have been taught to ignore the objection. When you call, what is the first question that you ask people? Is this a convenient time to talk? Twenty years ago, this was an act of courtesy. Today, it's a red flag that there's a salesman on the line.

Whenever I said, "No, this is not a good time," they would say, "It's only going to take a minute." So I have taken to giving them a very compelling reason why this is not a good time to talk. Now when I take in a call where somebody asks, "Is this a convenient time to talk for a moment?", I reply, "No I am sorry this is a very bad time because we are right in the very middle of having sex."

Three of these callers replied, "It's only going to take a minute." One lady apologized. The fifth one said, "I'll call back in five minutes."

☙☙☙

Here are some things you learn as you "mature":

- I've learned that you cannot make someone love you. All you can do it stalk them and hope they panic and give in.
- I've learned that it takes years to build up trust, and it only takes suspicion, not proof, to destroy it.
- I've learned that you can get by on charm for about fifteen minutes. After that, you'd better have a big weenie or huge boobs.
- I've learned that you shouldn't compare yourself to others— they are more screwed up than you think.
- I've learned that we are responsible for what we do, unless we are celebrities.
- I've learned that regardless of how hot and steamy a relationship is at first, the passion fades, and there had better be a lot of money to take its place.
- I've learned that sometimes the people you expect to kick you when you're down will be the ones who do.
- I've learned that we don't have to ditch bad friends because their dysfunction can make us feel better about ourselves.
- I've learned that no matter how you try to protect your children, they will eventually get arrested and end up in the local paper.

- I've learned that the people you care most about in life are taken from you too soon and all the less important ones just never go away.

❦❦❦

When I ran for provincial president of the Jaycees (Junior Chamber of Commerce), I found myself in competition with three other candidates. All of them had experience at the provincial level. Each of them spoke for the allotted time and then some. They knew everything that was wrong with our organization provincially. They knew all the negatives, and they told us about them. They offered few, if any, solutions. When my turn came to speak, the chairman of the meeting took me by the elbow and said, "Lyle, keep it short. We are already running overtime."

I started to protest. After all, I should have equal time with the others. I was the immediate past president of a very successful unit. I had prepared a very upbeat talk. "Forget the problems of the past. We are entering a new era."

However, I could tell that he was serious, and I knew that the audience was somewhat bored. So I agreed. I threw away my prepared talk, except for the following story:

One evening after a hard day's work, a father sat down to relax and to read the newspaper when his five-year-old son came into the room and asked his dad to play with him. The father told the child, "Not now, Daddy is busy."

But the kid kept on urging the father, "Please, Daddy, let's play."

Finally, the father, wanting to get the child off his back, got a great big jigsaw puzzle with a picture of the whole world, threw the pieces on the floor, and said to the boy, "Son, when you have put this together, we'll play."

Figuring it would take the child at least two hours to put the puzzle together, he went back to his newspaper. About five minutes later, his son said, "Daddy, I finished the picture, can we play now?"

The father looked down at the puzzle, and to his amazement, saw it complete. In great astonishment, he asked, "Son, how did you do it so fast?"

The kid answered, "Daddy, on the other side of the world picture is the picture of the head of a man, and when I put the head together, all was right with the world."

I concluded with, "If we work together, we could solve any problems, no matter what. Let's have lunch!"

Well, I won. I think it was due to that story. However, my friends Gord and Vern claim that their campaign efforts behind the scenes, with the voters, did the trick. They do admit, however, that the brevity of my speech made it the best one of the day.

❧❧❧

The following story is one that I can relate to. My wife tells me that I snore rather loudly. I tell her I don't believe her. I have never heard it. She threatens to tape-record it. So I make sure that she is asleep before I go to bed. I'm not suggesting that you go too far with this.

You may have heard about four guys who had fished together for years. They always got four separate rooms because Sam snored so bad. They didn't want to embarrass anyone, but nobody could sleep with him, so they just ordered four separate rooms. One year, they garbled the reservations at the fishing camp, and there were only two rooms available, with twin beds in each. They exclaimed, "Oh no, who's going to sleep with Sam?"

To be fair about it, they decided to draw straws, and the first morning his roommate came out looking terrible. He had bloodshot eyes and had hardly slept. The next night, it was another fellow, and he came out the next morning looking even more disheveled. "I didn't sleep a wink," he said. That man makes more noise than anybody I've ever heard. I shook him, tried everything, but couldn't get him awake."

So they were interested to see what the last fellow looked like, but he came out the next morning looking fine. He'd had a good night's sleep.

"You did?" they asked, "What did you do?"

"I didn't do anything." He said. "Well, one thing I did do. Just before we went to sleep, I reached over and kissed him goodnight, and you know, he sat up and watched me all night long."

❧❧❧

Recently, I heard a motivational speaker relate the following old story. It's been around for forty years or more, but I think you will like his version of it:

My field is communications and public relations. It's a very ancient, honorable field, and it shouldn't be put down as it often is. It so happens that it goes clear back into biblical times. Moses had his own public relations man. In fact, he had a full staff, as any good CEO would have. Pharaoh says the Jews could leave Egypt, then he changes his mind, pulls out the troops and has got the Jews trapped on the edge of the Red Sea. In the process, everybody's uptight, and Moses calls his executive staff into the executive tent. And he's feeling confident and gritty, and he says, "Have I got a super, spectacular plan. Wait 'til you hear this, fellas."

Like any good staff to the CEO, they're all a bunch of nit-picking boat-rockers whose job it is to tell him why it won't work. But Moses lays it out. "God has given me the power. I'm going to part the water. And I want you, then, to take our people across to the Promised Land. Now what do you think of that? If the Egyptians follow, the water is going to come in on them."

The first cat out of the bag is the doctor. He says, "I'm sorry, chief. Have you given any thought to how damp that's going to be with all the water? We'll have problems with pleurisy, pneumonia, emphysema, and the dead, decaying bacteria in the bottom of the Red Sea. By the time our people get across, they're going to be so disease-ridden the immigration authority will turn them around."

"Gee, hadn't thought about that."

He looks for help to his chief engineer who's sitting next to the doc, and he says, "Sorry, Moses, I go with the doc." Moses asks, "Why?"

The engineer says, "Have you thought about a wall of water that high? Do you know how many pounds per square inch pressure at the bottom? And you're going to have our people walking between those two walls! You do this, human resources will have you in court for thirty years."

"Gee, hadn't thought about that."

Moses looks over to his legal counsel, and he's standing there with his arms folded, just shaking his head.

The counsellor says, "Moses, as your lawyer, I advise against this move. It's better to face Pharaoh's wrath. You think you got trouble with the human resources group, wait until those people step one foot on the bottom of that Red Sea, the SPCA is going to have you in court for sixty years."

He's about ready to throw out the plan when he notices Manny, his PR guy sitting over at the end of the table, and he's bouncing up and down, grinning from ear to ear.

Moses asks, "Manny, do you like the plan?"

Manny replies, "Mo, baby, I LOVE it! You pull it off, I'll get you five pages in the Old Testament!"

❦❦❦

Have you ever attended a class reunion with your wife? If so, you may be able to relate to the plight of a fellow professional speaker. His wife is a few years younger than he is, and he discovered that he was actually closer in age to some of her teachers than to her fellow students. While he was drinking punch and eating cookies, he watched his wife reminiscing with her old boyfriends to the tune of the Beatles song "Yesterday." One guy was 6 foot 4 inches, well built, and very handsome. He was a little jealous. When she returned, he interrogated her. "I saw you standing with that guy. Did you go with him?"

"Yep," she replied. "Four years."

"That's too long to go with anyone in high school. Did you go to the prom with him?"

"Yes, and I went to the after-prom with him too," she replied.

"Well, let me ask you this. How close did you come to marrying this dude?"

She answered, "Well, if you hadn't oversold me I would have married him."

"Well, what does this clown do for a living."

"He owns a string of service stations here in town," she replied.

"Right on," he laughed. "If I hadn't showed up, you would be pumping gas instead of being married to one of the great speakers in the country."

"Wrong," she smiled. "On the contrary, he would be one of the great speakers and you would be pumping gas."

❦❦❦

When Dr. Powers returned for a class reunion, he met one of his teachers. She was really old. She was the type of teacher that expected her students to try hard. She was a tough taskmaster. We've all had teachers like her. You know the type. You would cross the road to avoid her attention; the type you remember in later years as the one who developed your character the most; that special one, who made you achieve somewhere near your potential. You may even remember fondly that you survived her classes and went on to become successful—because of her. Well, Dr. Powers approached his old teacher and asked, "Hi, do you remember me—John Powers? You taught me in eighth grade."

She studied him for a moment and finally smiled. Then she said, "Oh yes, John Powers. I'm sorry, all grades are final!"

❧❧❧

Lou Holtz is a very witty guy. He has coached several top-ten football teams. Lou claims that in high school he ranked 234 out of a class of 278. That didn't bother him until the principal pointed out that, comparatively, it was a rather stupid class overall. At college entrance, the registrar questioned his academic background. "You will probably flunk out."

"You don't think I'm very smart do you, Miss Loan."

"Lou, let me put it this way. Many people don't know what is going on, but you—you don't even suspect something is going on."

❧❧❧

Lou says, "Football is a simple game. When the opponent has a running play, come up. When they pass, go back. I promise you, once the ball is in the air, it will not change directions. Don't cover the decoy. Cover the receiver."

One of the players asked, "How do you know who the decoy is?"

Lou replied, "That's the guy they don't throw to."

❧❧❧

When Ohio State played in the Rose Bowl, O.J. Simpson was the star for the opposition, Southern California. Woody Hayes, Ohio State's head coach, discussed with Lou the best way to defend against O.J. The last thing Hayes said to Lou before the game started was, "Well, he'd better not score a touchdown."

In the second quarter, Southern Cal had the ball, first and ten on their own 20-yard line. O.J. took the hand-off and rambled eighty yards for a touchdown. Lou was very happy at that point that he was in the press box rather than on the sidelines with Coach Hayes.

At half time, as they walked into the locker room, Coach Hayes came running up to Lou, grabbed him by the throat, and hollered, "Why did O.J. go eighty yards?"

Not knowing what else to say, Lou babbled, "Cause that's all he needed."

ơơơ

Lou read a book called *Winning by Intimidation*. Lou says that it is possible to win through intimidation, but that's not the style he prefers. Many speakers who travel have had experience similar to the one Lou related. There was no room at the inn. Lou had been giving talks at this hotel chain for over six and one half years. On one occasion, Lou arrived at one of the hotels and stated, "My name is Lou Holz, and I've got a reservation."

The reservations jockey replied, "I can't find it."

Lou answered, "I've got my confirmation slip. Hurry up, I want my room."

The clerk said, "Sorry, I can't find it."

"That's your problem. If your inept, don't blame me; find my room."

The clerk was obstinate. "I don't think I'm going to let you stay here."

"But," Lou repeated, "you don't understand; I've got a confirmation slip."

The clerk replied, "And I don't think you understand; I've got the keys."

Lou was upset, but what could he do? The guy had the keys, and he wasn't giving them to Lou Holz. At 1:35 a.m., Lou had to find accommodation in another hotel.

The clerk had the keys, and he won with intimidation.

"However," asks Lou, "what did the clerk win? Since that time, I never miss an opportunity when speaking to a prestigious group to knock that hotel. Lou says, "You can win a lot of things, but you should just do what's right. Treat others as you'd like to be treated."

❦❦❦

Lou likes to relate a true story about Coach Vince Lombardi of the Green Bay Packers. Lou says, "Coach Lombardi is famous for his opening speech with his new football team."

Lombardi's opening words were: "Gentlemen, this is a football."

"What some people do not know," claims Holtz, "is that one of the linemen, Max Green, replied, 'Coach, can you go a little slower?'"

❦❦❦

One of Lou's favorite coaches to pick on is Mike Ditka. When Mike was coach of the Chicago Bears, he had a problem that he would just not give up on. It was a big problem—a guy named William Perry.

His full name was William "The Refrigerator" Perry. No matter what Ditka did, he could not get Perry down to the weight he believed was best for Perry, as a football player. At the end of one season, Ditka rented a cabin in Northern Wisconsin and hired a nutritionist to put together a diet specifically for Perry. Then Ditka announced to the press that he and Perry were going to that cabin for three months—just the two of them. One way or another, Perry was going to lose weight. The press followed up and discovered that, within three weeks, Perry had gained 195 pounds, and Mike Ditka was missing.

Witty retorts are sources of humor:

One of the greatest masters of repartee was Winston Churchill. He was always fighting with Lady Astor. One evening, when Churchill was particularly misbehaving, Lady Astor came up behind him and said, "Mr. Churchill, if you were my husband, I'd put cyanide in your coffee."

Churchill looked up at her and replied, "Madame, if you were my wife, I would drink it."

George Bernard Shaw, on the occasion of the opening night of his play, *Man, and Superman,* sent Churchill an invitation. "Sir, you are hereby invited to opening night of *Man and Superman*. You may bring a friend—if you have one."

Churchill fired back. "Sorry I can't make it for your opening night, but I would be delighted to attend on your second night—if you have one."

When the German chancellor visited Churchill just prior to World War II, he warned Churchill: "And this time we will have the Italians on our side."

Churchill remarked, "That seems only fair. We had them last time."

Churchill claimed that there were only two things more difficult than making a speech. "The first is climbing a wall that is leaning toward you. The second is kissing a girl who is leaning away from you."

❦❦❦

When I started my professional speaking career, I called the convention convener of a firm about their upcoming conference. I told him about my program and that simply, "I would like to speak to your group."

He said, "Lyle, you're not ready."

I replied, "Yes, I am; I've got my outline prepared and everything."

He said again, "You're not ready."

I said, "I've been practising in front of a mirror."

He said, "You're not ready."

I said, "I'll speak for free."

He said, "Now you're ready."

❦❦❦

Some of the stories I enjoy are those told by and about people from the Deep South. Here are a couple:

Zeb was sitting on the front porch with his son Zeke. Zeke suddenly piped up: "Dad, can I ask you a question?"

"Sure son, what is it?"

"Well, I was wondering, Dad, what makes them aireoplanes stay up there?

"Don't rightly know, Zeb."

Sometime later, Zeke asks another question: "Well, I was wondering Dad, what makes them old trucks pull them big trailers?"

"Don't know son."

A little more time passes. "Well, Dad, another thing I was wondering, how can them big heavy boats float?"

"Don't know son."

After a long pause: "Dad, you don't mind me asking all these questions do you?"

"Nope, how else you gonna larn?"

❦❦❦

Recently, I heard a modernized version:

The little boy asked his father, "Dad, why is the sky blue?"

His father replied, "I don't really know son."

"Well, Dad, why is the grass green?", inquired the young lad.

"Gosh son! I don't really know," he replied.

"Okay, Dad, but I was wondering, why is the sun yellow?"

"You know son, you got me there. I just don't know."

The inquisitive boy thought for a moment and then asked, "Gee, Dad, I hope you don't mind me asking all these questions?"

You know the reply, "Heck no, son. How else are you going to learn?"

Well now, I don't like the modernized version very much. You see, I can believe the story when it pertains to an uneducated hillbilly. But would a modern-day dad reply this way? Surely the proper answer to each of these questions would be, "That's a good question son, let's find out the answer together."

❦❦❦

Mandy and Rastus are famous characters from the old south. One story about them that I enjoy goes like this:

One day when Mandy and Rastus were in church, the minister was really letting it out. Mandy was sitting in the balcony—first row. Rastus was sitting in a pew on the main level with the other young men. Mandy was leaning on the railing totally engrossed in the minister's message. Suddenly, there was a commotion and a rustling of clothing from above. The preacher stopped and stated, "Don't nobody look up. Mandy's had a little slip and her clothes are a little in dishevelment. Anybody looks up, the Lord gonna strike him blind."

Rastus, covering one eye, turned quickly, looked up, and stated, "I'll risk one eye."

(One time, I told that story and nobody laughed. Then I realized my *faux pas*. I had covered one eye in demonstration, but I said, "I'll risk one ear.")

❧❧❧

How many of us have experienced humor of the *faux pas*? When I was president of the Calgary Jaycees, I had an experience that I shall never forget. We sold tickets on the "Pot of Gold" at the world-famous Calgary Stampede—"The Greatest Outdoor Show on Earth." As president, one of my pleasant duties was to escort the "Pot of Gold" queen and her two princesses to various events. It was my job to introduce Miss Pot of Gold and her princesses to the audience. They welcomed the people and made a pitch about the fifty-thousand-dollar gold bar. "You gotta buy a ticket to win!"

We had several appearances each day. On the fourth day, we had attended several events, and everything went off without a hitch—that is until we got to the grandstand, where about twenty-five-thousand people were watching the show.

Then something strange happened to me. It was not nerves, because we had been out there on three previous occasions. However, as I approached the mike, I realized that I could not remember the Queen's name. I could not ask her, "What's your name?" I knew it, of course, but my mind went blank.

So I departed from the regular program and introduced the princesses first. Then I announced, "And now ladies and gentlemen, 'Miss Pot,' Lorraine Stack." I was so relived that I had remembered her name just in time that I failed to deliver the proper title, "Miss Pot of Gold."

A titter started way over on the left of the grandstand and continued like a wave from left to right and erupted in raucous laughter from that large audience. I was embarrassed but Lorraine, bless her, saved the day. She stepped forward and to the delight of the audience said, "That's Miss Pot of Gold, Lyle. *Miss Pot of Gold!*"

Back to the hillbilly stories:

A hillbilly made his first visit to the big city. He stood in the lobby of a skyscraper looking at the changing numbers over the elevator. As he watched in fascination, the doors opened and a little old lady stepped into what looked like a closet. The lights flashed and the doors closed. A few minutes later, the doors opened and out stepped a beautiful young lady.

"Golly gee," the hillbilly exclaimed, "I shoulda brung my wife."

❦❦❦

Another hillbilly from the state of Georgia was speaking with the doctor just after the delivery of the family's ninth baby.

The doctor gave him some fatherly advice, "You know, James, the next time you feel like propagating, you should ask yourself if you can support another child."

James looked at the doctor and replied forthrightly, "You know, Doc, when I feel like propagatin' I feel like I could support the whole state of Georgia."

❦❦❦

The next story is about Clarence and Boudreaux. They lived across the bayou from each other, and they didn't like each other at all. All the time, they yelled at each other.

Boudreaux would shout, "If I had a way to cross this bayou, I'd come over there and pass my fist through you jaw—yeah!"

Clarence would reply, "Ha, just you try it."

This went on for years until the state finally built a bridge over the bayou.

"Now's you chance, Boudreaux," his wife Maria exclaimed. "You go over there and beat up Clarence like you say."

Boudreaux say, "Okay." And off he went. Part way across, he came to a sign, stopped to read it, and went back home.

Maria asked, "Why you back so soon?"

He answered, "I no change my mind about beat up on Clarence, but they got a sign on that bridge say "Clarence 13 ft. 6 in.""

How's that for corny?

❦❦❦

Not all colloquial humor comes from the Deep South. Some enjoyable stories come from new people from other countries living in our country. For example: Ollie and Lena.

Ollie and Lena, of course from Sweden, migrated to Canada at a time when they were required to do farm labor for one year. After the year was up, they moved to a nearby city and got jobs more equal to their abilities. They also bought a nice home in the suburbs.

The new lifestyle left evenings free, and Ollie got a bit restless after a while. One day, after dinner, he told Lena, "I think I should go out for a little walk." Lena agreed.

Well, each evening Ollie went for his stroll, and one evening he discovered the neighborhood pub. After a few weeks, Ollie began staying out later and coming in slightly inebriated. Actually, it got worse, and Ollie was coming home later and later and drunker and drunker. Finally, Lena decided, "I yust gonna to put a stop to dis." She locked the front door.

Ollie, in his state of inebriation was somewhat flustered. When he figured it out, he shouted, "Lena open da door."

No answer!

Ollie stepped back into the street and shouted, "Lena, you open the ding dong door or I'm gonna bust him off the hinges."

Lena opened the upstairs window and shouted, "You yust do dat an you gonna pay for it from your own money."

Ollie thought for a moment and then screamed, "Lena, you hopen the door now, or I yell yust so loudt all the neighbors can hear, 'I sleeped with Lena before we was married.'"

Lena shouted back, "You yust do that and I yell yust so loud, 'You vasn't the only vone.'"

I love it!

Humor in sports:

I am a sports fan. As a player, baseball was my favorite. I was a catcher on our local team, in Wheatley, a little town near Windsor, Ontario, way south of Detroit.

Yogi Berra was an all-star catcher with the New York Yankees. I never missed an opportunity to watch Yogi play in the Detroit stadium or on TV. He was truly a legend on the field. Yogi Berra was also a legend as a spokesman. Whenever Yogi or his equally legendary manager Casey Stengel spoke, I would listen with fascination. Both Casey and Yogi could talk in riddles.

They were both masters of the art of doublespeak. In fact, it's doubtful if either of them could explain the situation in plain English. One got the feeling that they understood each other, but no one else could do so. They were like two small children. You can't understand them, but they know exactly what the other one is saying.

They had a strange and wonderful relationship.

When Casey explained the cause of the loss to the Brooklyn Dodgers, it came out sounding like the Yankees had actually won the game. Or maybe he was indeed talking about a different game.

One evening, several years ago, Casey was presented with an award. He held it up and said, "Ladies and gentlemen, thank you very much. I really don't appreciate this, but I certainly do deserve it."

❧❧❧

Some of Yogi's comments are among my favorites of all time. For example, one time, Yogi said, "It's difficult to make predictions, especially about the future."

Another time, he said, "It ain't over till the fat lady sings."

Duh, Yogi; it doesn't even start until the lady sings. Also, Yogi, she sang for the Philadelphia flyers before hockey games. Your sport is baseball, Yogi.

In those days, pizza was a novelty. I know, I know! Most people reading this book think pizza has always been with us. You probably believe also that pizza comes from Italy. Not so! Pizza, as we know it, was created in the U.S.A.

The story is told that Yogi took his family to a famous New York restaurant that specialized in the new fad—pizza. They ordered a large anchovy pizza. Large in those days was sixteen inches. The waiter asked, "Mister Berra, how would you like it cut—sixteen pieces or thirty-two pieces?"

Yogi replied, "Oh, make it sixteen pieces. We could never eat thirty-two pieces."

Another Yogi statement, "You can see a lot by watching."

🐾🐾🐾

About a restaurant in New York, Yogi said, "Nah, nobody goes there anymore, it's always too crowded."

We may question Yogi's mental agility, but we all quote him sometimes. How many people know that it was Yogi who said: "If you don't know where you are going, you'll probably end up somewhere else"?

"It ain't over till it's over."

🐾🐾🐾

Some of you may know that Yogi managed the New York Yankees for a few years. George Steinbrenner, the owner of the Yankees, was a tough taskmaster, and he and Billy Martin had a hot relationship. After George fired Martin for the third time, he hired Yogi Berra. When Yogi was moving into his new office, he discovered a note left by Billy Martin that read, "To my successor." This note was attached to two envelopes, number 1 and number 2. The message on the envelopes read: "Open only in case of emergency."

Yogi went on about the business of managing the team, which promptly lost the first six games. Steinbrener went berserk. Yogi rushed to his office and opened envelope number 1. It read "Blame it on me."

Berra, called a press conference and blamed everything on Billy Martin. This diversionary tactic worked perfectly, and it got the owner off his back—for a while. Later, the Yankees lost seven in a row. Steinbrenner was livid. Yogi rushed back to his office and opened envelope number 2. It read, "Prepare two envelopes."

🐾🐾🐾

Yogi Berra was definitely a great American philosopher. He stated, "The key to success is to avoid making the wrong mistakes."

The Chicago Cubs have not won the World Series since 1908. When Yogi heard that, he stated, "Well, anyone can have a bad century."

A reporter asked Yogi, "How are things going for you?"

Yogi replied, "I'm straddling the other side of the fence right now."

Tom Seaver, Mets pitcher, asked Yogi, "What time is it?"

Yogi's answer, "You mean right now?"

Phil Rizzuto, "pepper-pot Phil," was driving to a banquet with Yogi. "Yogi, we're lost."

"Yeah," Yogi answered, "but we're making good time."

One time, Yogi excused himself for showing up late to a meeting with: "This is the earliest I've ever been late."

A photographer asked Yogi to look straight into the camera.

Yogi stated, "I can't do that. That's my bad side."

❦❦❦

Here are some things Yogi might have said:

- If the strike isn't settled soon, it may last a while.
- War dims hope for peace.
- Cold waves are linked to temperatures.
- Something went wrong in the jet crash.
- Death causes loneliness and a feeling of isolation.
- At a feast of ego, everyone leaves hungry.
- It's hard to make a comeback if you've never been anywhere.
- This game is 90 percent mental and the other 10 percent is mental.

❦❦❦

Another baseball story tells about two fellows who had grown up together. They had played little league, high school, and sandlot baseball together. They agreed that when one of them died, he would come back to let the survivor know if they played baseball in Heaven. Well, one of the pair died, and the survivor waited to hear the news. After several weeks, the survivor went to bed, and in his dream the other fellow appeared. He said, "I've got good news, and I have bad news. The good news is that they *do* have baseball in Heaven. The bad news is that you are scheduled to pitch next week."

At least he had a little warning!

☙☙☙

I think you will enjoy the story about a rookie outfielder who was playing in his first professional baseball game. The manager of this team had been cautioned to give this lad lots of attention because of his great potential.

The team was ahead one to nothing in the last of the ninth with two out. The batter hit what should have been a game-ending fly ball to left field. The rookie was anxious to do well. He ran in quickly but realized he should have run out. He desperately ran back. The ball hit him between the shoulder blades and fell to the ground. It was a three-base error.

The manager was not thrilled. He sat in the dugout and fumed.

The next batter hit a lazy fly ball to left field. This should have been a game-ending fly ball. The rookie, anxious to redeem himself got right over there, camped just right. The ball hit the heel of his glove and fell to the ground, for another three-base error. A run scored. The game was tied, and a runner was on third base. The manager erupted. He stormed out of the dugout and said, "You dumb rookie. Get to the bench. I'll show you how to play left field." Sure enough, the next batter hit a fly to left field. The manager ran over and flipped down his sunglasses. But, in his anger, he ripped too hard and the glasses went slant-wise across his face. He lost the ball and made an error.

The game was lost.

The manager went running into the dugout and right after the rookie. He fumed, "You dumb rookie. You got left field so screwed up nobody can play out there."

☙☙☙

What do ants have to do with golfing? Well, one of the less-than-average golfers in the local golf club missed the ball more often than he hit it. Sound like anyone you know? This fellow kept digging up dirt to the point that he had the sharpest clubs in town. On the fourth hole, his ball landed on an anthill. It didn't bother him. He just squared off, swung through, and killed a few thousand ants. He swung again, missed the ball, but killed a few thousand more ants. He kept on swinging until the whole ant colony was destroyed. It was the greatest ant massacre in history. Ants were dying everywhere.

Two ants walked out of what was left of the hill, and one said to the other, "You know if we don't get on the ball, we are going to die too."

There is a moral here for everyone. If we want to survive, we better get on the ball.

❦❦❦

My favorite sports story is about Maurice Richard. Some younger people may not know that Maurice, "The Rocket," was a legendary hockey star with the Montreal Canadiens. Maurice scored fifty goals in fifty games. There was another great star playing for the Detroit Red Wings while Maurice played with Montreal. Maurice retired, but the tireless Gordie Howe continued to play.

One evening, on Hockey Night in Canada, in a game between Detroit and Montreal, the Rocket, was the "color man." Danny Galvan was the announcer. Maurice, the Rocket, did a tolerable job, and he was asked to pick the three stars after the game.

"Well, for the first star, I would have to choose my brudder, "the Pocket Rocket." Tonight, he skate like the wind, and he score the first goal that put us in front."

Danny Galvan stated that he thought that was a good choice, and asked, "How about the second star?"

"For duh second star, I would say Jean Belliveau. He is such a good playmaker. He set up two of the goals that we scored tonight."

"Certainly a good choice," replied Galvan. "No one could question Belliveau's value to his team. Now, how bout the third star?"

"Duh tird star, I pick Jacques Lapperiere. He is such a good defenceman. If it wasn't for Jacques, you never would know how many goals dose guy with Detroit might have made."

"Well," says Danny Galvan, "Those are all very worthy choices, but let me ask you if you would have an honorable mention?"

"A honorable mention?" queried Maurice. "Oh sure, I suppose so. For duh honorable mention I would say that big guy, you know, Gordie Howe, that scored the four goals that beat us."

❦❦❦

Boxing fans know Cassius Clay by the adopted moniker of Mohammed Ali. Ali went around introducing himself as the most beautiful fighter in the world. He would say, "I have speed and endurance. If you fight me, increase your insurance. I don't ask what boxing can do for me. I say what I can do for boxing. I'm so fast that when I get ready for bed and turn out the light, I'm in bed before it gets dark."

When Mohammed Ali was boxing champion of the world, he was traveling in the first-class section of a commercial jet. A few minutes before takeoff, the flight attendant came by and asked Ali to fasten his seat belt. Ali told her, "Superman don't need no seat belt."

The flight attendant paused momentarily and then said, "Superman don't need no plane either."

Cash flow is what goes out but never comes in!

Do you like humorous signs? There is a sign on the wall of one of our favorite restaurant's that reads:

> God made earth and rested.
> God made man and rested.
> When man rested, God made woman.
> Since then, neither man nor God has rested.

On a billboard in Quesnel, British Columbia, there is a sign that says: "All those who hate speeding tickets raise your right foot."

Other signs:

- *On a gate:* "Cemetery road—no exit."
- *On an electrician's truck:* "Let us remove your shorts."
- *On an optometrist's office wall:* "If you don't see what you are looking for, you've come to the right place."
- *On a hotel's wall:* "Help! We need inn-experienced people."

- *On the front door of a home:* "Everyone on the premises is a vegetarian, except the dog."
- *On a fence:* "Salesmen welcome. Dog food is expensive."
- *On an office wall:* "We shoot every third salesman. The second one just left."
- *On a post in a non-smoking area:* "If we see you smoking, we'll assume you are on fire and take appropriate action."
- *On the door of a muffler shop:* "No appointment necessary. We will hear you coming."

What are the last words
you want to hear when you are making love?
"Hi honey, I'm home."

When I was writing this book, my wife told me I shouldn't tell dumb blonde jokes. She's blonde with a bit of gray here and there, but it's difficult to notice it unless you look closely. Blonde women do have some advantages.

My hair is black with a lot of white thrown in. If you look very closely, you can see a hint of black, somewhere.

Anyway, I said, "Why not? Dolly Parton likes dumb blonde jokes."

"Okay, but your not Dolly Parton."

"Yeah, and neither are you."

"Just what did she say, anyway?", my curious wife queried.

Dolly said, "I don't mind dumb blonde jokes because, first of all, I know I'm not dumb."

"Also," said she, "I know I'm not blonde."

❦❦❦

There is a restaurant where Betty and I dine frequently. We know the owners well, but, most important, the food is great and the service is special. All of the waitresses are blonde. However, I suspect that some of them have had a little help from Clairol.

One day, our waitress brought my tea, as always, then came back for our order. I said, "Linda, what color is tea?"

"Oops, I forgot the tea bag." And she rushed away to get it.

When she returned she stated, "It's Edna's fault. She hires too many blondes around here."

❦❦❦

When I told my blond wife the following blonde joke, she managed a snicker:

A young man wanted to get his beautiful blonde wife something special for their fifth wedding anniversary. He bought her a cell phone and carefully explained all the features on the phone. She loved it. The next day when she went shopping her phone rang, and it was her husband. "Hi Hon, how do you like your new phone?"

"I love it," she replied. "It's so small but your voice is clear as a bell. There's one thing I don't understand though."

"What's that love?"

"How did you know I was at Wal-Mart?"

Just after I showed that story to my wife, she got her new cell phone. One morning, when I left for the office, Betty went to her eye examination. Without her at the office, I was lost. There were some files I could not find. Suddenly, I thought about the new cell phone and called her. She told me at once where to find the files. Then she asked, "Tell me, how did you know I was at Lenscrafters?"

Touché.

❦❦❦

Huguette Lawson, another blonde (maybe), also likes blonde jokes. She contributed the following one:

A guy was having a drink in a very dark bar. He leaned over to the big woman next to him and asked, "Do you want to hear a funny blonde joke?"

The big woman replied, "Well, before you tell that joke, you should know something. I'm blonde, six feet tall, 210 pounds, and I'm a professional triathlete bodybuilder. The blonde woman sitting next to me is 6 feet 2 inches, weighs 220 pounds, and she's a professional wrestler. Next to her is another blonde who is 6 feet 5 inches, weighs 255 pounds, and she is currently a kick-boxer. Now, do you still want to tell that joke?"

The guy thought about it for a moment and then replied: "Nah, not if I'm going to have to explain it three times."

❦❦❦

Huguette also contributed the following:

- If a messy kitchen is a happy kitchen, my kitchen is delirious.
- No husband has ever been shot by his wife when he is doing the dishes.
- A clean house is a sign of a misspent life.
- Keep your kitchen clean—eat out.
- Housework done properly can kill you.
- If we are what we eat, then I'm easy, fast, and cheap.
- A balanced diet is a cookie in each hand.
- Thou shall not weigh more than your refrigerator.
- Countless numbers of people have eaten in this kitchen and gone on to lead normal lives.
- A husband is someone who takes out the trash and tries to pretend that he has just cleaned the whole house.
- My next house will have no kitchen—just vending machines.

ஃஃஃ

A blonde who was terribly overweight went to her doctor about it, and he prescribed a diet. "I want you to eat regularly for two days and then skip a day. Then repeat the procedure for two weeks. The next time I see you, you will have lost at least five pounds."

When the blonde returned, the doctor was amazed to discover that she had lost over twenty pounds.

"Why that's amazing," the doctor exclaimed. "Did you follow my instructions?"

The blonde nodded, "I'll tell you though, I thought I was going to drop dead on the third day."

"From hunger you mean," the doctor queried.

"No, from skipping," she replied.

How's this for disappointment?

When I got married, I expected I would have sex any time I wanted it. I lived with that expectation for almost three days.

Talking about non-rewarded expectations. When the doorbell rings, our dog always runs to the door barking and with her tail wagging. It's never for her, but she does it again next time anyway.

A sign on a wall in Las Vegas, "*A Smith & Wesson still beats four of a kind.*"

❧❧❧

If you have trouble meeting people, try picking up the wrong golf ball. One time on a public golf course, I hit my ball into the rough close to another fairway. I saw a ball and leaned down to inspect it more closely. A woman shouted at me, "Hey, mister that's my ball."

It was scuffed and cut and thoroughly beat up. I laughed and replied, "You got that right. I throw balls away that look better than that one."

She neither blinked nor smiled. She just pushed me out of her way and said, "Yeah, we can't all be rich."

Happiness is contagious. Be a carrier!

Some professions claim they make better lovers:

- Cowboys stay on longer.
  (Eight seconds?)
- Scuba divers like to go deeper.
  (Try kissing one in gear.)
- Truckers are in for the long haul.
  (They're always pushing knobs and turning dials.)
- Doctors do it with physical aplomb.
  (They're always probing for something.)
- Dentists like to drill it.
  (It's the sound that rattles you.)
- Lawyers do it legal.
  (Dull.)
- Accountants can do it without losing their balance.
  (They count every stroke.)
- Surgeons do it with precision.
  (When they're done, you don't notice any marks.)

- Mechanics can make it more powerful.
  (But they're always revving their motors.)
- Professional drivers do it faster.
  (But they're always spinning wheels.)
- Geologists know where the fault is.
  (They're always looking at crevices.)

❧❧❧

Dr. Eliot, an U.S. cardiologist, has some interesting observations:

- There are no perfect idiots, but there are some that come pretty close.
- When someone throws you a ball with guilty written all over it, where is it written that you have to catch it?
- Play has four powerful components: freedom, spontaneity, whimsy, and laughter.
- Don't sweat the small stuff. It's all small stuff!

Dr. Eliot also said:

Is there a stress carrier in your life? Suppose I told you that person has a brain tumor. And it's the mechanical pressure exerted by that brain tumor against the mind that affects the way they react towards you. Medicine can't help it. What would you say if you knew it was a brain tumor, a mechanical thing producing that change? About 85 percent of the people surveyed said, "Well, gee, I'd feel a little sad."

The other fifteen percent said, "I wish the darned thing would grow faster."

But the point is this: If someone acts toward you as if they had a brain tumor, why treat them as if they didn't?

Keep that in mind. The next time that happens and your favorite stress carrier comes along, just say, "Here comes old Homer with the brain tumor again. How can he help it?" It's a way of slipping life's psychological karate chops and a very powerful way of doing it.

The secret of life is learning how to hit the curve ball, not waiting until life quits throwing curves.

Learn to say "I'm sorry." Learn to say "I love you."
Hardly a day goes by that my wife doesn't say,
"I'm sorry I love you!"

Tom Sullivan is an actor, a pianist, a singer, an entertainer, and a motivational speaker. He is blind. He claims that before he was married he went out on a lot of blind dates.

He wonders about signs that say, "No Seeing-eye dogs allowed. Who is going to read them?"

Tom likes to play sports. In little league, he was a pitcher. He only lasted one inning. Nobody would bat after he beaned the third batter to face him.

Tom swam competitively. He wrestled internationally. He even tried tennis. He could serve all right, but if his opponent hit the ball back, it was game over.

Finally, Tom took up golf. According to him, he is good. In fact, he challenged Arnold Palmer. When he met Palmer at a golfing event, Tom stated that he had always been a fan. Palmer replied that he was a great fan of Tom's also. Tom told Arnold that one of his dreams would be to play a round of golf with him. Arnold stated, "You know, Tom, I have never played with a blind golfer, but it would be a pleasure to play with you."

"Great," replied Tom, "But there is one thing. I like to wager when I play."

Arnold chuckled, "Well, sure, Tom. What did you have in mind?"

"A thousand dollars a hole."

"Whoa, Tom, a thousand dollars a hole? Tom, you know that golf is my avocation and my vocation. Some people say that I'm pretty good at it."

"That's okay," says Tom. "I insist on one thousand dollars a hole."

"Well, Tom, if you insist, we will play any place you want, any time."

"Wonderful," Tom quipped, "Here, tonight at midnight."

❧❧❧

Barry Asmus, Ph.D., has a few thoughts on politics and politicians:

Divide the wealth; spread it about; sharing is no sin.
When mine runs out, I plan to shout: "Let's divvy it up
    again."

Their palms are soft; their grip lacks clout.
Yet they win votes with each handout.

If two people agree on everything, one isn't needed.

Hear about the old lady who walked into the judge's chambers unannounced and asked, "Are you the judge of reprobates?"

He replied, "Well, I'm the judge of probates."

"That's it, I 'spect," answered the old lady. "You see," she went on confidentially, "my husband died *detested* (intestate) and left me several *infidels* (infants), and I want to be their *executioner*."

Did you hear about the university that has been using lawyers as guinea pigs for all testing programs instead of monkeys, rats, cats, or rabbits? The reasoning is, there is an unlimited supply and you do not become attached to them.

There is a cartoon with about thirty lawyers on a beach, buried in sand up to their necks. *Caption:* "What's wrong with this picture?" *Answer:* "Not enough sand."

The sequel—picture of a ship loaded with lawyers. The ship is sinking slowly into the sea. *Caption:* "What's wrong with this picture?" *Answer:* "Not enough lawyers."

Phyllis Diller once quipped, "My mother-in-law is so big that, when she wore a gray suit, an admiral boarded her."

We are constantly being advised that, if we want to improve efficiency, we should make "to do lists!" Reportedly, Phyllis Diller has several lists. On one of them, the first item was, "Pick up Cher's new boyfriend from day-care school."

☙☙☙

Try starting your talk with the following:

Hi, my name is Lyle, and I'm an alcoholic—Oh, wrong room? Let me start over. Hi, my name is Lyle, and I'm a salesman—Uh, this isn't sales anonymous? Right, and you would prefer the alcoholic?

☙☙☙

Sometime ago, I attended a sales conference with my company in Toronto. After the formal evening meeting, we all retired to a company-provided room for the rest of the evening. Several people told jokes. I decided it was my turn and started to tell about the Shakespearean troupe that had just arrived in town. While I was talking, I noticed that some people had stopped just outside the open door, and they could hear everything.

No problem, I continued with my report.

The troupe arrived to discover that their advertising material had not made it. They had to come up with something quickly and cheaply that would explain about the six plays they planned to present. It would have to be on one sheet of paper.

At this point, one of the people from the hallway approached me and asked, "Could you tell us where Kenneth Moore is staying?"

I assured them that I did not know Kenneth Moore. I did not know Roger Moore (007), and I did not know Dudley Moore (entertainer and movie actor). I would not know Kenneth Moore if he walked in. Of course, I knew that he was a Shakespearean actor, but I had no idea that he was actually in Toronto. He had nothing to do with the story I was telling. I told them I was only telling a joke, and I invited them in to listen to the rest of it.

One of my *buddies* piped up and said, "Oh, Lyle, they look like nice people, I'm sure you can tell them where he is. I don't think he will mind."

Great, just what I needed. I assured them that my friend was joking. I tried to convince them that I really did not know anything about Kenneth Moore. They left, somewhat reluctantly, not quite believing me, thanks to my friends. We all had a good chuckle, and I completed my story.

Later, as we broke up to retire, Peter, who had been so helpful, suggested that we should have a nightcap in the lounge before going to bed. Three of us went down to the lounge. There were two sides, with a bar in the middle. Except for us, the entire place was empty. We chose a table in the middle of the room on the left. We ordered, but before our drinks were delivered, Peter, my helpful friend said, "Guess who is standing at the door?" Thinking it was our new friends from upstairs, I looked over to discover just one man.

"There," said Peter, "is the Kenneth Moore."

Kenneth Moore could have chosen the room on the right, which was empty, but he chose the side we occupied. He could have sat at a table well away from us, but he chose the one right next to ours.

Peter leaned toward him and said, "Mister Moore, I'm a great fan of yours. I have seen you in several Shakespearean plays in England."

Kenneth Moore registered surprise, but he was obviously pleased. Peter told him which plays he had seen, and when and where he had seen them. They struck up a conversation, and Peter asked him to join us at our table. He did.

As we were discussing whether Kenneth preferred stage or screen, several other people came in and took up tables all around us. The room was now filled. Obviously, these people were actors from the Shakespearean troupe.

We were engrossed with Kenneth Moore's tales about his acting experiences. Suddenly, I noticed the little group of people from upstairs. The very ones I had tried to convince that I did not know Kenneth Moore. They spotted him and came right over to our table. I kept my head down. There was no point in trying to explain it now. Obviously, I had lied.

Well, they never got to hear the end of the story, but you may have it now if you wish.

The imaginary troupe with the advertising problem printed one sheet to do their task. It read:

3 inches
6 inches
10 inches
Miscarriage
Wet
Dry

That's it. You should now know which plays they planned to perform. Okay, I'll tell you, but a joke that needs to be explained is at it's wits end:

3 inches = Much Ado About Nothing

6 inches = As You Like It

10 inches = Taming of the Shrew

Miscarriage = Love's Labor Lost

Wet = Midsummer Night's Dream

Dry = Twelfth Night

I'll bet those people still wonder why I lied to them.

❦❦❦

Bar Room Humor:

You can't fool your wife. Can't be done!

One night, a patron of a nearby neighborhood bar believed he had had enough to drink, so he decided to go home. When he stood up, he slipped and fell to his hands and knees. After a couple of unsuccessful attempts to get up, he gave up and decided to crawl home. His home was not that far away.

On hands and knees, he succeeded in reaching his front lawn, then up the steps to his front door. Several attempts later, he managed to get the door open, and he crawled in kicking the door shut. He rested for a time at the foot of the stairs leading to his bedroom. Finally, he gained enough strength to navigate the stairs and collapse exhausted into his bed. In his inebriated condition, he fell into a deep sleep.

He was awakened next morning by the ringing of the telephone. Moments later, his wife appeared at the foot of his bed. "You got a bit drunk last night, didn't you?", his wife chuckled.

"Humph," he replied in a bit of a huff. "Why do you say that?"

"Well, dear, that was the bartender on the phone. You left your wheelchair in the bar."

Another man was out drinking and had too much. He had a bottle in his hip pocket, the remains of the evening. He got to his house all right, just three steps from the front door. He made one shot at it and stumbled back. He went at it again, stumbled, and fell on the bottle. It broke, and, even in his condition, he knew that medical attention was in order. This time, he crawled up the steps, went into the downstairs bathroom, backed up to the mirror on the door and made the necessary repairs. He sneaked out of the bathroom, went upstairs, and crawled into bed. Success! He did not wake her.

Next morning, he went down to breakfast. His wife greeted him with, "You got drunk again last night, didn't you?"

He denied it. "I was out a little late, but I was not drunk."

His wife smiled knowingly, "Well, what are all those band aids doing on the bathroom mirror?"

Nope, you can't fool them. Don't even try!

❧❧❧

Two other old guys left the bar slightly tipsy. They decided to walk home along the railroad. After slipping and sliding around for a while on the loose gravel, they moved to the railroad ties. About a half-mile later, one of the guys huffing and puffing said, "This is better; isn't it?"

His drunken partner, totally out of breath, replied, "Yeah, I don't mind climbing these steps so much, but these low hand rails are getting to me."

❦❦❦

Another of the buddies at the bar struggled to his home. Part-way up the steps to his bedroom, he slumped down huffing and puffing like a beached whale. His concerned wife, who had heard his noisy entrance, hollered to him to come on up to bed.

"I can't right now," her rather stoned husband replied.

"Well, why not? You're half-way up already."

"I know, but I just can't manage it."

"Why not, are you that drunk?"

"No," he stated emphatically. "But I'm carrying a barrel of beer."

"Well, leave it. You can take care of it tomorrow," she snarled at him.

"I can't do that," he puffed, "it's inside me."

The golden rule:
He who has the gold makes the rules.
Do unto others, then split.
Do unto others before they do unto you.

One of my friends, Lorne, is an inveterate golfer. He has been known to miss appointments because an opportunity to play golf came up and he forgot everything he was supposed to be doing. His wife Maria found this bit of irresponsibility somewhat infuriating. Lorne was otherwise a model husband and father. But a chance to golf was too much for him to resist. To avoid marital confrontation about his golfing activities, which continually interfered with promises made, Lorne learned to become somewhat evasive. This was a well-known fact to most of his friends. Nevertheless, this new style did not fool his wife nor did it ingratiate him to her in any way. Not surprisingly, a friend brought this trait up on the occasion of a wedding anniversary party. He told the friends assembled about an incident that had taken place recently between Lorne and his wife:

One day last week, Lorne arrived home late for dinner. He had neglected to pick up the kids after school, and he had completely forgotten some errands. Lorne wanted to explain what had happened. "Maria, we need to talk. I have something to tell you of great importance."

Maria said, "Not now, Lorne, the kids are hungry. We'll eat first."

After dinner, she said, "Wait till the dishes are done and the kids are in bed."

Finally, they sat down together with a glass of wine. Maria allowed, "Okay Lorne, what is the excuse this time?"

"It's no excuse, dear, and I cannot believe what happened today. I know you will be angry, but I hope you can forgive me. It's not something I planned. It just happened."

"Oh well, Lorne, let's hear it then."

"Well, Maria, you know Nancy, my secretary, has been working really hard to get the proposal for the condominium job finished. And finally, just before noon, it was completed. To reward her efforts and to celebrate its completion, I took her to lunch. We went to a nice secluded Italian restaurant where we had a lovely meal with lots of wine. We just lost track of time. It was too late to go back to work, so I drove Nancy home. When we got to her house, she suggested that I come up for a coffee. Well, one thing led to another, and we ended up in bed. I didn't mean for it to happen. We just lost control. I hope you can forgive us."

Maria looked at him disdainfully and snarled at him, "Oh, Lorne, you lying bastard, I know you were out golfing."

Here's a tall tale from Calgary:

When we first came to live in Calgary, it was much colder during the long winter months than now. However, oldtimers loved to tell us how much colder it used to be when they were young. They used to get much larger snowstorms. Chinook winds were much more powerful. One old boy told me, "When I was a young lad, an old farmer was driving his snow cutter to town. He looked over his shoulder and noticed a Chinook arch forming in the west. He shook the reins to get his team to walk faster. Half a mile further, he noticed that the wind behind him was picking up quite a bit. He slapped his team gently with the reins. They responded with a slow trot. Still, a little later, he felt the warm wind swirling around his cutter. He slapped the horses' rumps, and got them into a full-paced run. When he got to the edge of town, the team was running as fast as possible on the snowy roadway. As he looked around, he saw that the front runners of the sleigh were running in snow while the back runners were kicking up a dust storm." What a memory!

❦❦❦

Two atoms collide. One atom says, "I think I lost an electron."
  Second atom, "Are you sure?"
  First atom, "Yes, I'm positive."

❦❦❦

Have you heard about the guy who had ten brothers and sisters when he was growing up? He never slept alone until he was married.

So you want to tell your story; right?

If you have ever spoken to a group where some of the people in the audience know as much about your topic as you do or more, you may be able to relate to the following tale. You may feel like the survivor of the terrible Johnstown flood of 1889.

One survivor made quite a name for himself, traveling all over the country telling about his experience. He spoke to huge crowds wherever he went. Eventually, he died and went to Heaven. As soon as he arrived in Heaven, he began urging St. Peter to assemble the heavenly host so they could hear his flood speech. After a while, St. Peter relented.

  St. Peter said, "All right, we've reserved an auditorium for you and I'm sure every seat will be filled. But there is something you ought to know. One of the people in the audience will be a fellow by the name of 'Noah'."

❦❦❦

He was a very cautious man
Who never romped nor played.
He never smoked, he never drank,
He never kissed a maid.

And when he up and passed away,
His insurance was denied.
For since he never lived,
They claim he never died.

How's this for powers of observation?

Sometimes, traffic on the freeway can be hectic. One day, a young lad, who was tailgating, finally got around my car. I noticed a sign on his bumper that read, "Honk if you know Jesus." So I blew my horn and he gave me the finger—the single digit salute. One of my acquaintances explained it to me, "Nah, he's just saying that you are number 1 in his books, or maybe it was a borrowed car."

Amateurs teach amateurs to be amateurs!

Sherlock Holmes and Dr. Watson were camping in the forest. They had gone to bed, and they were lying beneath the night sky. "Watson, look up; what do you see?"queried Holmes.

"I see thousands of stars," Watson commented.

"And what does that mean to you?", Holmes asked.

"I suppose it means that of all the planets in the universe, we are truly fortunate to be here on Earth. We are small in God's eyes, but we should struggle every day to be worthy of his blessings. In a meteorological sense, it means we'll have a sunny day tomorrow. What does it mean to you, Holmes?"

"To me, my dear Watson, it means that someone has stolen our tent."

❧❧❧

Writing on a tee shirt: *"If I had known I would live this long, I would have taken better care of myself."* (The guy wearing it was about thirty years old.)

❧❧❧

About the great late John Savage—a mentor to many during his illustrious career! John claimed that he had two million dollars of life insurance on his life. "You've got to own it before you can sell it."

He told his wife, "No laughing at the funeral. Wear something black and keep your head down."

He explained, "It's tough being unhappy when you know that in two weeks you're getting $2,000,000."

John always carried two thousand dollars cash with him.

"John, that's foolish; you could get robbed."

John chuckled, "That's why I carry it. Can you imagine some guy following me around, coming up with a gun and saying, 'Give me all your money.' I give him $2,000, and he's happy. Happy people don't shoot."

John claimed, "Eighty-two percent of the chemistry in your brain is dedicated to emotion. Only eighteen percent is dedicated to thought. That's why there is not much thinking going on."

"Some people claim that they would rather work than play." John's reaction to that was, "Obviously, they have never played."

The trouble with doing something right the first time is that, nobody appreciates how difficult it was!

Goal setting!

In nearly everything we do, we are advised to set goals. One of my friends, on his sixty-fifth birthday, set a goal for how many times he would like sex in the coming twelve months. At the birthday party held in his honor, he announced to those friends present, "My goal is to have sex seventy-five times in the next year." Then he turned to his wife of many years and asked, "How many of those would you like dear?"

Practical studies!

A rich man mentioned that he had a son still in college after six years. A friend asked him what he was studying.

"Women," came the reply.

The friend chuckled, "How did he do?"

"He flunked. But now he's going to summer school in Europe."

"Oh really?" inquired the friend. "What will he study there?"

"European women!", the dad quipped.

"What will he be when he graduates?", his friend queried.

"An old man!", retorted the harried father.

About government funding!

When Chris Columbus sailed to America, he didn't know where he was going. When he arrived, he didn't know where he was. When he went home, he didn't know where he had been. All he knew was that he was on a government-funded expense trip. And even with this inane report he was able to get the government to support him on a second all-expenses paid trip.

Oscar Wilde once quipped:
"Education is admirable, but let us not forget that anything worth knowing cannot be taught!

Lee Trevino's golfing philosophy is "be relaxed." Lee, one of the all-time great golfers, is quite a character. He likes to have fun when he golfs with friends. One time he quipped, "I used to be a poor Mexican. Now I'm a rich Spaniard."

He sometimes asks his opponent, as they are addressing the ball, "Do you breathe in or out on your back swing?"

In a pro-Am tournament one year, Lee's amateur partner asked for advice on several occasions. On the fifteenth hole, the amateur made two back-to-back great shots that put him on the green about thirty feet from the pin. If he could make the putt, he would birdie the hole. He looked it over carefully, then asked Trevino, "How should I play this shot?"

Lee just smiled and replied, "Try to keep it low!"

Perspective:

A shoe salesman was sent from the east out west. Immediately he wired, "Cancel supplies. Everybody here wears boots."

A second salesman was sent to the same territory. He wired, "Double my order. Great opportunity! Everyone here wears boots."

☙☙☙

Of course, there is another side to perspective. For instance, consider the story of daddy's little girl living away from home for the first time in her life. She was enrolled in the University of Arizona. After three months, she finally wrote to her parents. They excitedly tore open the envelope. The letter read:

Dear Mom and Dad

I've been remiss in writing and I'm sorry for my thought-lessness. I'll bring you up to date. But before you read on, please sit down. Don't read any further unless you are sitting down.

I'm getting along pretty well now. The skull fracture and the concussion I got when I jumped out of the window of my dormitory, when it caught fire shortly after my arrival, is pretty well healed now. I only spent two weeks in hospital. Now I can see almost normally, and I only get sick from headaches once a day. Fortunately, both the fire in the dormitory and my jump were witnessed by an attendant at the gas station near the dorm. He called the ambulance and the fire department. He also visited me in the hospital on several occasions.

After I was released from the hospital, I had nowhere to live because of the burned-out dorm, so my new friend invited me to share his apartment. It's a basement room, but kind of cute.

He is a very fine boy, and we have fallen deeply in love, and we are planning to get married. We haven't got an exact date yet, but it will be before my pregnancy begins to show. Yes, Mom, Dad, I am pregnant. I know how much you have been looking forward to becoming grandparents. I know you will welcome this baby and give it the same love and devotion and tender loving care you gave me when I was a child. The reason for the delay in our marriage is my boyfriend has a minor infection that prevents us from passing the blood tests. You see, I carelessly caught it from him.

Well, now that I have brought you up to date, Mom, Dad, I want to tell you there was no dormitory fire. I did not have a concussion or a fracture. I am not in the hospital. I'm not pregnant. I am not infected. I am not engaged. There is no boyfriend in my life.

However, I am getting a "D" in History and an "F" in French. I wanted to put things in perspective.

Love, Donna

Mark Twain observed, "Everyone talks about the weather but no one does anything about it." He also noted, "If a cat steps on a hot stove, it will be the last hot stove it will ever step on. And it will be the last cold one too."

There is no ship like friendship!

A husband came home one day to find his wife packing. He asked her, "What's up?"
   She gleefully told him, "I won the lottery."
   "Great! Where are we going?", he asked.
   "You didn't hear me right, I said *I* won the lottery!

The Lone Ranger Rides Again!

When I was a kid, we used to listen to this radio program as often as possible. Who was that masked man with the silver bullets, and how about that friendship with Tonto? Well the following story sheds a little light on that question:

The Lone Ranger, who rode out of the west to do good deeds had a constant companion named Tonto. One day as they were riding through the west, they were suddenly surrounded by about five hundred Comanche Indians. The Lone Ranger looked at Tonto and said, "Looks like we're in real trouble here."
   His supposed friend, Tonto, replied, "What do you mean, 'we,' white man?"

Lotto Prayer:

   As I lay me down to slumber,
   All I need is one more number.
   And if I pick the winning ticket,
   I'll go to my boss and tell him where to stick it.

❦❦❦

Ball Washer

Okay, son, I've got a mouse. Now what do I do?

A lad who was in desperate need of a large amount of money for a worthy cause, decided to pray for divine intervention:

"Please, God, let me win the lottery." Silence! But the lad kept praying. Finally, he got an answer. "Give me a break. At least buy a ticket."

Obesity!

A lady went to a doctor about her obesity. She weighed 325 pounds. She told the doctor, "Obesity runs in my family."

The doctor replied, "Nobody runs in your family."

❧❧❧

You know you are fat when: You look like a refrigerator with a bowling ball on it. You get your shoes shined and you have to take the guy's word for it. Your feet disappear when you step up to address the golf ball.

❧❧❧

There was a really fat guy in grade nine. Naturally, he was somewhat shy about being seen naked in the boys' locker room. Everyone had been instructed to buy certain equipment for gym class. One of the items for boys was a jock strap, known as an athletic supporter. Unfortunately, the fat boy did not know what it was for. He did not know how to put it on, and he was too embarrassed to look at the other boys. In his experience, labels on clothes meant that the label goes to the back. That's the way he put it on. Afterwards he wondered what it supported.

❧❧❧

Actuaries are mathematicians who calculate probabilities. They are all the same except for nationality differences. For example: A North American actuary can look at a room full of people and tell you how many are going to die. The Sicilian actuary can supply names and addresses.

❧❧❧

Clients!

A client told the salesman, "I can't stand you."

The salesman replied, "I wish I had fifty clients like you."

The client queried, "Are you crazy, man?"

"Oh no, I've got a hundred clients like you. I wish I had only fifty."

There are two people I can't stand and you are both of them.

Speaking!

How many speakers have wondered why they were selected for a particular program? If they were brave enough to ask, they may have experienced the following:

"Why did you select me as your feature speaker for today?"

"Because your cheap."

One time, my introduction was, "We invited Joe Gondolfo to speak to us today, but he did not respond, so I called Lyle and threatened him with some old information I have about him. So here he is."

However, that wasn't the worst of it. I was already slightly unnerved before the introduction when the ways and means chairman made an impassioned plea for an increase in annual dues. He stated, "If we had more money, we could afford to get better speakers."

I felt like quoting Groucho Marx, "Before I speak, I've got something important to say."

Imagine a speaker walking into a large room to speak and there is only one person there. What do you do? You could break the 100-yard dash record to the nearest exit, or you could say to yourself, "Wait a minute, I'm in sales. I'm here to communicate. Even if I can help this one person it will be worthwhile."

You start your speech and, after two minutes, the one young man sitting in the audience moves up to the front row. "Hey that's great!"

Five minutes into your talk, the young man is clapping his hands. Five minutes more and he is clapping enthusiastically.

By the time you are finished, the young man is on his feet giving you a standing ovation. You rush from the podium, walk up to the enthusiastic young man, shake his hand, and ask if there is anything else you can do for him?

He smiles and says, "Oh yes, would you please sit down right here? I'm the next speaker."

Many speakers travel thousands or even millions of miles each year. They can probably relate to this story about Justice Oliver Wendell Holmes:

At the turn of the last century, Justice Holmes boarded a train in Boston. Soon after leaving the station, the conductor came around collecting tickets. Justice Holmes searched his pockets—his trousers, his jacket, his vest, but he could not find his ticket.

The conductor recognized the distinguished Supreme Court justice. He said, "Justice Holmes, don't worry about your ticket. I'm sure you will find it when you get home. Just mail it back to us. There is no problem."

Justice Holmes, continuing to go through his pockets, retorted, "My good man, the ticket isn't the problem. The problem is: Where am I going?"

One speaker I heard opened his talk with, "My role in this event, I'm told, is a lot like being the corpse at an old-fashioned Irish wake. It's necessary to have me there in order to have a party, but nobody expects me to say much."

Have you ever moderated a panel discussion with several highly distinguished speakers? It can be somewhat intimidating. One of my associates took care of that problem by making a statement to the audience. The panel members were well-known highly successful businessmen. Also, they were good friends of the moderator. Before he made the introductions, he explained his role to the audience.

"The duty of the moderator is to be so dull and boring that the speakers will appear brilliant by comparison. Well, I've looked over the list of speakers for this morning, and I don't believe I can do the job."

Many speakers state emphatically and with conviction that, "You never get a second chance at a first impression." That seems like a fairly obvious observation. However, first impressions are not really as important as they claim! If first impressions were so important, fewer of us would be married.

If you're a workaholic and you finally catch up to the Jones's, you know what will happen. They refinance!

On Driving!

Don't you just love driving behind some elderly people? Well, it may have been fun to follow this lady as she drove her friends to a meeting in another town. This dear elderly lady was driving thirty miles an hour on Interstate 30. The speed limit was 75 miles an hour. A patrolman sitting on the side on the highway noticed the car puttering along. He thought to himself, "That's just as dangerous as speeding." The officer turned on the lights and stopped the driver to see why she was driving so slowly.

He noticed that there were five other ladies in the car, and they were as white as ghosts. The elderly lady driving was somewhat confused about being stopped. She asked, "Officer, I don't understand. I was doing exactly the speed limit. Why did you stop us?'

"Ma'am," replied the officer, "You weren't speeding, but driving much slower than the speed limit can also be dangerous to other drivers."

"Slower than the speed limit?", she challenged. "No sir, I was doing exactly the limit, 30 miles an hour."

The officer contained his chuckle as he patiently explained that "30" was the route number, not the speed limit. At that, the lady was a bit embarrassed as she grinned and thanked the officer for pointing out her error.

"Before I let you go, Ma'am, I need to ask, if everyone in the car is okay. These ladies seem a little shaken, and they haven't uttered a word while we've been talking."

The elderly lady driver stated, "Oh no, they will be okay in a minute. You see, we just got off Interstate 119.

ʚʚʚ

Ugliness versus beauty!

There are some advantages to being ugly. If you women marry a good-looking man, he might leave you. If you men marry a beautiful woman, she may leave you. Of course, an ugly man or woman might leave you also, but who cares.

Are you clairvoyant?

Once upon a time, there was a man who had extremely smelly feet. He used two pairs of odor-eaters per week. It was so bad that he had to wash his feet with his shoes on. He met a lady with halitosis. Her breath was so bad that she had to use industrial-strength mouthwash. They fell in love and got married. As he carried her over the threshold, she whispered, "There's something I've got to tell you."

He replied, "I already know. You don't have to tell me. You ate my socks, right?"

❧❧❧

Another couple fell in love and decided to marry. He told his beloved that he had a confession to make. "I am an inveterate golfer. I golf three times a week and every weekend, no matter what."

She said, "That's okay. We can manage that, but I have a confession. You see, I'm a hooker."

"No problem," he replied. "We can work on your stance and change your grip to correct that."

Overcoming objections!

In my forty-five years as a salesman, I have heard every objection to buying life insurance. At least, I thought that I had heard them all until recently. One guy told me, "I don't believe in life insurance. When I die I want it to be a very sad day. I want it to be a real tragedy."

❧❧❧

He had heard about another guy who left $1,000,000 in life insurance proceeds. The guy's widow stated, "I miss him so much; I'd give $10,000 to have him back."

We often hear the concept,
"Work smarter, not harder."
Well, I have found that the smarter I work,
the harder I work!

Did you know that the first life insurance ever issued in North America was written on December 15, 1792? According to Pamela Yellan, the policy was written by the "Insurance Company of North America," in Philadelphia. It was issued on the life of Ebenezer Hazard. Mr. Hazard died just seven months later. That's fairly common knowledge, but no one ever says anything about the beneficiary. Who inherited the proceeds of that first policy?

It turns out that a favorite nephew, Zeboriah Heap, inherited the entire $600 when his uncle passed away. Fortunately for us, there is a record of what happened to the money because nephew Zeb liked to keep a journal of his activities! In it, he wrote, "Inherited $600 from uncle Eb; went into town; spent $200 on hard liquor; $200 on sightly women, and $200 I squandered." (This is fact, partly based on fiction.)

Choosing the right word!

The words we use and your reaction to them are a matter of choice. Another way of saying it is this: The word you use is not the thing. It expresses a sentiment and we react accordingly. I am not trying to justify foul language by suggesting that it is your reaction that is at fault, but sometimes a four-letter word expresses the sentiment so well. Some people avoid the use of such words and phrases by substituting other more socially acceptable expressions. For example, they say:

"Doll golly" instead of "Damn it all!"
"Son of a biscuit," not "Son of a bitch."
"Dag nab-it" or "darn it," instead of "Damn it."
"Holy cow," instead of "Bullshit."

And so on. What they are actually trying to do is express the feeling attached to the more fiery words while appearing to be above the use of the words generally associated with the sentiment. They know that we understand what they're trying to imply. The listener substitutes the implied concept mentally, and that is supposed to make it more palatable. But, let me remind you, the speaker is trying to elicit the feeling while avoiding the actual words or phrases normally used on the street. What the hell difference does it make? Who are they trying to kid?

When I wrote this, I showed it to my wife and admitted, "I really enjoy an opportunity like this to take people to task for such linguistic idiosyncrasy."

She replied. "I know, Lyle, when you're right, you can be a real pain in the ass."

Shakespeare said:
"There is nothing either good or bad,
but thinking makes it so."

Esther was always a bit outspoken. She tended to be rather blunt when she told it like it is. Not only was she a bit direct, but she used some colorful expressions that were not becoming of a young lady. So her parents sent her to a finishing school for young ladies. She was supposed to learn proper etiquette.

About ten months later, she returned, and, on her first trip downtown, she met some of her old high school chums. The first one was Linda, who she had always thought of as a bit of a bore. Linda showed her a sparkling diamond ring and announced that she had met the most wonderful guy. She claimed that he was vice-president of one of the largest firms in the area. Linda went on and on about him *ad nauseam*. Esther curtailed her natural tendencies and replied as expected of a young lady. "That's marvelous, simply marvelous."

Just then, they met Margaret, who told Linda and Esther all about her new job. She claimed that she was being promoted over many of the others, even though they had much more seniority. Her bragging irritated Esther, but she maintained her decorum, replying with, "Why that's marvelous, simply marvelous."

Finally one of the pair asked Esther, "What about you? What have you managed to learn at that fancy finishing school? Have you learned anything useful at all?"

"Oh yes," replied Esther enthusiastically. "At charm school, they taught me to say, 'Marvelous, simply marvelous,' instead of 'bullshit.'"

❦❦❦

Another chap I know was in litigation with a fellow who had cheated him on a financial matter. His lawyer advised him that the opposing lawyer would attempt to get him angry and goad him into saying things that should be avoided. This lawyer was quite young and rather arrogant. Frequently, the lawyer lectured my friend in a rather supercilious manner. My acquaintance merely replied each time with, "Thank you, sir."

After the session, his lawyer complimented him on his ability to maintain his composure. She stated, "I was quite surprised that you did not retaliate with a verbal outburst on several occasions. Congratulations!"

"Oh, it was not difficult," he replied. "First of all, I envisioned him sitting there across from me in his underwear. Secondly, I decided that every time he provoked me, I would say 'Thank you sir' rather than 'f—k you!'"

❦❦❦

One guy I know decided to eliminate all "swear" words from his colorful language. He lost 50 percent of his vocabulary.

Aging!

One fellow said, "If I take that five-year course, I'll be sixty-three years old when I graduate."

"No kidding, if you don't take the course, how old will you be five years from now?"

By the way, how old would you be, if you did not know how old you are?

My mother was suffering some arthritic pains and she told me, "Lyle, don't ever grow old."

"Whoa, Mother, are you saying I should die young?"

Winston Churchill said:
"Winning is never final. Losing is never fatal!

After I had beaten one guy thirty years my junior in three straight sets of handball, he came up to me and said, "Gee, it must really be tough getting old." I grabbed him by the shirt collar and replied, "Well it's a lot better than the alternative."

☙☙☙

An elderly lady took the college course entry exam to see how smart she was. Her scores were very high and several universities solicited her to enroll in law school. She was flattered, but suddenly she realized that if she did take the course she would end up as a lawyer. She enrolled in psychology instead.

Never put off until tomorrow what you can do today!
If you enjoy it today, you can do it again tomorrow.

A swimming experience!

A wealthy eccentric gentleman invited a number of eligible young men to meet his marriageable daughter. In his swimming pool, he had several large alligators. "Here's the deal, men. If any one of you is brave enough to swim the length of the pool with all the alligators in there, I'll give you a choice of three things.

1. My daughter's hand in marriage.
2. One hundred acres of prime land.
3. $100,000.

No sooner had he finished the offer than he was surprised to hear a loud splash. The young man in the pool swam with alacrity and made it to the other end before the alligators could get him. The rich eccentric was impressed.

"You win," he exclaimed. "What will it be? Do you want my daughter's hand in marriage?"

"No," exclaimed the out-of-breath lad.

"Then you want one hundred acres of prime land, no doubt?"

"No!"

"Okay, then you shall have the $100,000."

"No," exclaimed the youth.

"Well, if you don't want anything I have offered, what do you want?"

The young man snarled, "The name of the guy who pushed me in."

How's this for logic!

At the top of Sulphur Mountain in Banff, Alberta, it was noticeably colder than at the bottom of the gondola. A young lad asked his father why it was so cold. His father replied, "Because we are on top of a mountain."

"Yes," answered the child, "but we are a lot closer to the sun, so it should be warmer."

"Okay, Dad," I thought to myself, "I want to hear your answer to that bit of logic."

Imagine being judged by a jury of your peers who were not smart enough to get out of jury duty!

One time when I was making phone calls to prospective clients, I got a wrong number. A young-sounding lady answered the phone, and I asked for George.

She stated, "There's no George here."

I consulted my list and the phone display to see if I had dialed incorrectly. Since it was the number I dialed, I asked, "is this 233-2558?"

"Yes, that's correct," she confirmed.

"And George Jones doesn't live there?" I queried.

Her brusque reply was, "Look, have I ever lied to you before?"

If everything's under control, you are going to slow!

Shortly after Ken Taylor, a Canadian diplomat in Iraq, helped some American's escape through the Canadian embassy, my wife and I were vacationing in Acapulco, Mexico. We were waiting in line in a lounge area when somehow it was mentioned that we were Canadians. Several very lovely, young American ladies left their male escorts and lined up to kiss me squarely on the lips.

They commented, "We can't thank you Canadians enough for what you did for us."

Well, even though I had nothing to do with it, I was more than a little willing to accept thanks on behalf of Ken Taylor. My wife observed this affectionate display for a moment and then exclaimed, "Hey, I'm a Canadian too."

The escorts promptly rose and rewarded Betty with equal passion. It was a good evening for Canadians.

How about the guy who refused to make love to his wife, but shot the guy who did?

I've been a life insurance salesman for most of my working life. The companies I worked with routinely rated bartenders for having a hazardous occupation. There did not seem to be a good reason for it, so I wrote to the company's chief underwriter:

Dear Bob

We have just submitted an application on the life of Joe Brown, using standard rates. Under the circumstances, I feel that we should not rate this individual. First of all, he is a non-drinker. In fact, he has never drunk alcohol of any kind. Secondly, he is a non-smoker, and he has never smoked. He does not do drugs of any nature. He does not keep a gun behind the counter, and, furthermore, he does not have a knife for defensive purposes. On the occasions that I have visited this lounge, I have noticed that the patrons are businessmen and women, lawyers, accountants, salespeople, and visitors to our fair city.

Some of the people who frequent this establishment are clients of your company, and they all received insurance coverage at standard rates. All of them were drinking, and some of them were smoking, and, for all I know, some of them may be acquainted with things stronger than liquor.

Our applicant is a happily married family man, and he attends church regularly. He works out on a regular basis at the YMCA. In fact, that is where I met him. He has never had an altercation with any patrons in his work place, because it is a high-class establishment.

It's true that Calgary is known as a frontier city, but we have never had a shoot-out at "ye olde corral." We do not check our guns at the door, because we do not carry guns. Gun laws in Calgary are very similar to those laws common to Toronto. It seems logical that, if you can underwrite the clientele of this establishment without rating those who do imbibe, you should be able to offer standard coverage to one who never partakes of the evil essence of grape. Surely, you cannot argue that serving your clientele this substance is a more serious than using it.

Sincerely,

(After passing the letter around head office for a chuckle, they issued the policy at standard rates.)

ଷଷଷ

There was a sign on the bulletin board, in a sales office for all the salespeople to see. It read: "Lonesome? Like to meet new people? Like to travel? Like excitement? Like a new job? ... Then screw up one more time!"

Another sign on the bulletin board read: "Firings will continue until morale improves."

ଷଷଷ

A guy asked his wife what she wanted for Christmas.
She replied, "A divorce."
His answer was, "I wasn't planning on spending that much."

ଷଷଷ

One day, a guy looked over his fence and asked his neighbor why he was digging a hole.
"To bury my canary," was the reply.
"Do you need a hole that big for a canary?", the neighbor asked.
"Yeah," the one digging the hole puffed, "She's inside your cat."

The patrons of a local lounge were quite pleasantly surprised to discover that the attendant was offering: beer at 5 cents a liter, chips at 5 cents a bag, chocolate bars for 5 cents each, and so on. One of the regular clientele asked, "Where is the owner?"

"Upstairs with my wife."

"What's he doing upstairs with your wife?", the patron queried.

"Same thing as I'm doing to his business."

(If you think that's bad you should hear some of the ones that didn't get past the censors.)

☙☙☙

My neighbor informed me that his wife was finally learning to park the car in their garage. He stated, "Last night, she backed the car in and this morning she backed it out."

I am an optimist.
I don't see how things could get worse!

A parrot was watching a thief pilfering from a store. The parrot perched nearby started shouting "Jesus is watching; here Moses, come Moses."

This attracted the owner, who came over and accosted the pilferer.

Caught red-handed, the thief asked, "Why does your parrot say, 'Jesus is watching.'"

That's the parrot's name—Jesus."

"I don't believe it," commented the thief.

"Then you probably don't believe that Moses is a Rottweiler, and he is right behind you."

☙☙☙

"Where's your dinner?", asked the cook."

"I gave it to the dog," the man replied.

"Oh no," replied the cook.

"Don't worry, I can get a new dog in the morning."

Sign on the wall:
"Don't worry about the dog. Worry about the owner."

An acquaintance of ours owns a store where he sells specialty products. He has a sign on the wall as you enter. "Beware of dog." Every time I have been in the store, his old Labrador was asleep on the floor, and he did not even take notice of my presence. On one occasion, I asked Fred about it, "Why do you need a sign warning about this lazy old dog?'

Fred laughed, "Before I put that sign up, people were always tripping over him."

❦❦❦

"Dad," the young student asked, "I'm doing a report on the war. How do you spell NATO?"

"U.S.A.," answered the father.

If bulls had no horns, we would have no matadors!

A man ordered two dozen roses to be sent to his beloved on her twenty-fourth birthday. His card read, "A rose for every precious year of your life."

Then, because the young fellow was one of his best customers, the florist threw in an extra dozen.

❦❦❦

Smart son: "Dad, I siphoned a couple of gallons of gas from your car for my old bus. It's okay, isn't it?"

Smarter father: "Sure it's okay son. I bought the gas with your allowance for next week. So, run along and have a good time."

❦❦❦

An old mountain man found a small mirror, the first he had ever seen. He looked into it with surprise and said, "By cracky, it's a picture of me old pappy." Sentimentally, he hid the mirror under the bed.

His wife saw him hiding it and when the man left the house she took the mirror, looked into it, and snorted, "So that's the old hag he's been chasin."

❦❦❦

A chaos of clear ideas!

Pascal said of one of his opponents, "He dwarfs great things by dint of bringing them within reach."

☙☙☙

A woman said, "What I cannot forgive him for is his having made me understand so many things that I shall never understand."

Voltaire said, "Sages retire into solitude and become sapless with ennui."

How's this for ignorance?

The bumblebee's body is so heavy and its wings are so light that it is aerodynamically improbable for it to fly. But the bumblebee doesn't know it.

☙☙☙

A confused farmer was standing in a field with a rope in his hand. He could not remember if he had just lost a cow or found a rope.

☙☙☙

My friend Chris Herdzig contributed the following:

My name is Bob and I am a Canadian.

I am a minority in Vancouver, Banff, and in every casino in this country.

I was born in 1972, yet I am responsible for some Native's great-great-grandfather who lost his land in the 1800s.

I pay import tax on cars made in Ontario.

I am allowed to skydive and smoke, but not allowed to drive a car without a seat belt.

All the money I make until mid-July must go to paying taxes.

I live and work among people who believe Americans are ignorant about our geography.

But these same people cannot name this country's new territory.

Although they are unpatriotic and constantly try to separate, Quebec still provides my nation's prime ministers.

Ninety-five percent of my nation's conflicts are over fish.

I'm supposed to call black people African-Canadians, even though I'm sure none of them have ever been to Africa, or east of Halifax, for that matter.

I believe that paying 200 percent tax on alcohol is fair.

I believe that same tax on gasoline is also fair.

Even if I have no idea what happened to that old rifle my grandfather gave me when I was fourteen, I will be considered a criminal if I don't register it.

I often bad-mouth the United States, and then vacation there three times a year.

I am led to believe that some lazy-ass unionized broom-pusher who makes $30 an hour is underpaid and therefore must go on strike but paying $10 an hour to someone who works twelve-hour shifts at forty below on an oil rig is fair.

I believe that paying $30 million for three stripes (The Voice of Fire) by the National Art Gallery was a good purchase, even though 99 percent of this country didn't want it and will never see it.

When I look at my pay stub and realize that I take home one third of what I actually make, I say, "Oh well, at least we have better health care than the Americans."

I must bail out farmers when their crops are too wet or too dry, because I control the rain.

My national anthem has versions in both official languages, and I don't know either of them.

Canada is the highest taxed nation in North America, the biggest military buffer for the United States, and the number one destination for fleeing boat people.

I am not an angry white male. I am an angry broke taxpayer.

My name is Bob, and I'm a Canadian!

Growing old gracefully!

You know you are getting old when getting some action means you don't have to take a laxative. Getting lucky means finding your car in a parking lot.

As George Burns said, "When you bend over to tie your shoe laces you look around to see if there is anything else you can do while you're down there."

You know you are getting old when your best new friend is the pharmacist. It takes longer to rest than it took to get tired.

Having Alzheimer's is not all bad. After all, you can plan your own surprise party. You can hide your own Easter eggs. You can even meet new people every day without even leaving home.

❧❧❧

A comedian pointed out that, according to some scientists, some day in the future, people could live to be 140 years old. Reflecting on that thought, he said it didn't bother him that much that at age 120 he might be responsible for his parents who would then be 140 years old. What really disturbed him was that his 100-year-old child might still be living at home.

The war between the sexes will never be won. There is too much fraternization with the enemy!

When a friend of ours reached age ninety, she decided that she no longer wanted to live alone and maintain the family home. With her family's help, she moved to a home for senior citizens. There she met a widower who was not quite eighty-seven years old. They became good friends and spent many enjoyable hours together reminiscing about the years gone by.

On the evening of the day that the elderly gentleman turned eighty-seven, he came to our friend's apartment to play whist. In the middle of one game, the old gent suddenly said, "Today is my birthday. Guess how old I am. Bet you can't do it."

She looked at him for a moment and said, "Take off all your clothes."

"What?", he asked somewhat surprised.

She repeated, "You want me to guess your age, so take off all your clothes."

With a bit of a wry smile, he did just that.

She instructed him, "Now turn around slowly."

When he had done so, she looked him over carefully. Then she stated, "You're eighty-seven."

"How could you tell that?", he queried somewhat skeptically.

With a prankish grin she replied, "You told me this morning at breakfast."

Later in the week, the ladies' auxiliary held a masquerade party. Everyone was supposed to dress up in costume. The eighty-seven-year-old friend showed that he had a sense of humor. He took off all of his clothes (again) and streaked the party. He went as a dried flower arrangement.

❦❦❦

A minister was visiting one of the eldest men in the senior citizens home. The old boy said, "Yep, I'm ninety-eight years old, happy, healthy, and I haven't got an enemy in the world."

That's wonderful, the minister commented, "Congratulations! That's a beautiful thought and a wonderful achievement. After all these years— no enemies."

"Yeah, I outlived them all."

❦❦❦

These stories tell me that we can and should have a sense of humor throughout our lives. Of course, you can't wait until you are ninety to find it. A good sense of humor can sustain you in any situation. Having a sense of humor is sexy. When men are asked the characteristics they find most appealing in women, they list humor in the top five. When women are asked to name the things they find most attractive about men, having a sense of humor is always included in the top three, and quite often it is number one. Being aware of your sense of humor can actually enhance your love life. If you and your lover have the same sense of humor, good or bad, you greatly improve your chances of having a good relationship. So if you and your lover are in bed laughing together, that's a good sign. If, however, only one of you is laughing, that's a different matter.

Laughter and sex are two of the best stress-cycle breakers known to the human system. It doesn't matter whether they're 1, 2, or 2, 1, but if they come together—well that's a sign that you are getting old.

❦❦❦

What's to worry?

A young lady, Marian, was permitted by her parents to take a job in a large city and live in her own apartment. The one condition was that she would not allow male friends in her apartment as that would worry her mother. During a long-distance phone conversation with her mother, Marian described her date of the previous evening.

"You didn't take that man back to your apartment, did you?", queried her nervous mother.

"Oh no," answered the dutiful daughter, "we went back to his apartment. Let his mother worry."

❧❧❧

That's my Grandpa!

When my maternal grandparents celebrated their fiftieth wedding anniversary, my Aunt Shirley coerced me to say something or play the piano or whatever. At first, I declined, but she told me that my brothers Grant and Elwood had both agreed to say a few words. So naturally I felt compelled to do my part.

Grandpa was a man with a very small build. He was very quiet, and in my experience he never scolded a child no matter what. Grandma was the disciplinarian. She had a large frame, and she could leave an impression on your backside if you failed to obey her commands. I doubt seriously if Grandpa ever argued with his dear wife. Everyone present knew that he was very mild-mannered. He was adored by his family and friends.

Everyone who spoke before me talked of how much our grandparents had done for them. It was touching to hear the wonderful things they had done for us.

Of course, I could have added a few examples of my own, but I decided to take a different tack. I told the audience of family and friends, "Most of you know that Grandpa just got home from a convention in Toronto. What you may not know is that he and his two traveling companions were stranded in London because of the big snowstorm. After some time, they were able to find a motel with two rooms. The other two agreed to share one room, leaving Grandpa on his own. As they finished signing in, a young lady approached the counter and pleaded for a room. She was advised that the last two rooms had just been let. She was in a state of mental turmoil. She had been everywhere in the city, and there was not a room to be found.

The clerk was sympathetic, but there was nothing he could do.

"Surely," she begged, "you could find a bed for me somewhere. I am very tired. I have been driving all day, and I cannot go on in this weather."

The young lad was exasperated. "Ma'am, the only extra bed in the entire motel is in Mr. Smith's room." (His name was Leslie Smith. No kidding.)

The young lady, Linda Jones (kidding), rushed to grandpa and pleaded, "Mr. Smith, I am desperate. Could you let me use the extra bed in your room?"

After a moment of indecision, Grandpa gave in and asked the clerk to install a divider of some sort between the two beds. Miss Jones was very grateful. Grandpa quickly got ready for bed and crawled between the covers. "Goodnight, Miss Jones. Sleep well."

Miss Jones rustled around for a bit, then she too slipped quietly into her bed. "Goodnight, Mr. Smith."

All was quiet for a while. Grandpa was almost asleep when he heard, "Oh Mr. Smith, it's a bit stuffy in here. Could you open the window a crack?"

Grandpa's bed was nearest the window, so he dutifully complied. Again there was peace, and Grandpa was nearly asleep when Miss Jones asked, "Mr. Smith, now it's getting cold. Would you mind closing the window?"

Ungrudgingly, Grandpa did as he was asked. For the third time, just as he dozed off, Miss Jones interrupted, "Mr. Smith, could you get me a glass of water?"

Now Grandpa was fully awake. After a moment, he said, "Miss Jones, how would you like to be Missus Smith for the night?"

Without hesitation Miss Jones replied, "Why, Mr. Smith, that's a great idea."

"Okay," replied Grandpa enthusiastically, "Then get you own damned glass of water."

People who laugh at the boss's jokes may not have a sense of humor, but they surely have a sense of direction!

Very funny, Scotty.
Now beam down my clothes!

Education at it's best!

Father Guido Sarducci (of Saturday Night Live) once proposed a new university. It was to be an accredited degree-granting university. You could attend for five minutes and get a full degree. Sarducci was sure that he would be allowed to grant degrees because of the way he was going to teach the various subjects. He planned to teach it to students over age forty who did not go to university when they were younger. He would teach them what those who had attended remembered, twenty years later. For example:

> Spanish one: "Buenos dias."
> Spanish two: "Como esta usted."
> Economics: "Buy low—sell high."

❦❦❦

One morning, Al Gore and Governor George Bush, when both were presidential candidates, had a meeting over brunch in a restaurant. An attractive waitress asked Gore what he would like. He replied, "I'll have a bowl of oatmeal and some fruit."

"And, Sir, what can I get for you?"

Bush replied, "How about a quickie?"

"Governor Bush," the shocked waitress replied, "How rude and your not even President!"

As the waitress stormed away, Gore leaned over and whispered to Bush, "It's pronounced *quiche*."

Time is nature's way of keeping everything from happening all at once. Space is necessary so it doesn't all happen here!

Have you ever needed an interpreter when you were speaking? A number of professional speakers have had the experience of speaking to a group where an interpreter was required. They can relate no doubt to the American general who spoke to a large crowd in an Asian country. He did all the right things. He spoke clearly and slowly and allowed plenty of time for the interpretation. After a while, things were going well, so he decided to tell a joke. It took several minutes to set the scene and to delivery the punch line.

The interpreter spoke one line, and the audience erupted in laughter. The general was curious as to how his joke could be told so quickly. He asked the interpreter, "What did you say?"

The interpreter replied, "I told them American general tell funny story. Everyone laugh now."

☙☙☙

One speaker I heard about was speaking to a large audience in Latin America. He wanted to greet his audience in Spanish with "Good morning, ladies and gentleman." He knew how to say "Good morning," but he wasn't sure about "ladies and gentlemen." However, being an enterprising type, he looked at the restroom doors. When he stood before the audience that morning, he spoke with his most articulate Spanish, "Good morning, ladies and gentlemen." The audience laughed, and that made him think his enunciation must be off. He visualized the phrase and, holding off his interpreter, said it again. This time, the audience howled uncontrollably. He was about to try it again when his interpreter, who was in hysterics himself, came up to him and asked, "What are you trying to say?"

"I'm trying to say, 'Good morning, ladies and gentlemen'."

"That would be a good thing to say," allowed the interpreter.

Somewhat exasperated now, the speaker asked, "Well, what precisely am I saying?"

The interpreter, hardly able to contain himself, answered, "You are saying 'Good morning, bathrooms and broom closets.'"

☙☙☙

Henning Arndt, a client of mine, sent this one to me:

On July 20, 1969, Neil Armstrong, commander of the Apollo 11 lunar module, was the first person to set foot on the moon. Everyone knows his words that were televised to Earth and heard by millions, "That's one small step for man; one giant leap for mankind." But only a few heard the enigmatic remark he made just as he re-entered the lunar module, "Good luck, Mr. Gorsky."

Many people at NASA thought it was a casual remark to some rival Soviet cosmonaut. However, on checking, they could find no Gorsky in either the Russian or American space programs. Over the years, many people questioned Armstrong as to the meaning of his comment, "Good luck, Mr. Gorsky." But Armstrong only smiled.

On July 5, 1995, in Tampa Bay, while answering questions following his speech, a reporter brought up the twenty-six-year-old question. This time, Armstrong finally responded. Mr. Gorsky had died, so Neil felt he could answer the question.

In 1938, when Armstrong was a kid in a small mid-west town, he was playing baseball with some friends in the backyard. One of the boys hit a fly ball which landed in his neighbors yard near the bedroom windows. His neighbors were Mr. and Mrs. Gorsky. As he bent to pick up the ball, he heard Mrs. Gorsky shouting at Mr. Gorsky, "Sex! You want sex? You'll get sex when man walks on the moon."

❦❦❦

Calgary hockey has not been the best recently, as the Calgary Flames have missed the post-season playoffs for several years now. Calgary and Edmonton are great rivals, usually. Well, Edmonton fans love to poke fun at Calgary when their teams are even slightly better. This story comes from the self-described city of champions. They claim that two Calgary Flames fans died in an auto accident and ended up in Hell. In spite of the heat, these stalwarts wore ski jackets. The devil asked them how they could stand it? They replied, "Well, it was so cold in Calgary that we really appreciate the warm weather here."

So the devil turned up the heat and checked back to find these lads in light jackets hosting a barbecue to celebrate the nice weather. For some reason, that disturbed the devil so he cranked the temperature down to freezing level. Everyone in Hell was suffering from the blizzard. "That will teach them," stated the devil. The devil then returned to see how the Calgary fans were reacting to the new conditions. To his consternation, he found them in their parkas, "tuques," and warm mittens, dancing around gleefully celebrating, yelling, and cheering like madmen.

The devil was dumbfounded. "I don't understand, when I turned up the heat you were happy. Now it's freezing and you're still happy. What's wrong with you guys?"

The Calgarians were surprised at the devil's question.

They replied, "Well, don't you know, if Hell freezes over, it means the Flames have won the Stanley Cup."

Thanks Edmonton! Your turn's coming.

❧❧❧

Christina Herdzig sent another gem. She was laughing so hard she could hardly type it:

Four men went golfing one morning. One of the foursome went into the clubhouse to arrange the tee-off. The other three headed directly to the first tee. They started bragging about their sons' successes. The first one claimed, "My son is a home builder. He is so successful that he gave a friend a new home for free."

The second contributed, "My son started as a car salesman and now he owns a multi-line dealership. He is so successful that he gave a friend a brand new Mercedes, fully loaded."

The third man, not to be outdone, bragged, "My son is a stockbroker, and he is doing so well he gave his friend a stock portfolio."

When the fourth guy joined them after taking care of business, one of the originals on the tee mentioned, "We are just talking about our sons. How is your son doing?"

"Well," replied the fourth, "my son is gay and he dances in a gay bar."

The other three grew silent until he continued. "I'm not totally thrilled about the dancing job, but he must be doing well. His last three boyfriends gave him a house, a new Mercedes, and a stock portfolio."

Thanks, Chris.

Economists!

Several years ago, a Nobel prize winner, in economics was invited to Washington to deliver a major address to Congress. The demand was so great to hear him they had to move out of Congress and into JFK Stadium. As he was being driven down the New Jersey Turnpike, headed for Washington, he rehearsed his speech. His chauffeur turned to him and said, "Boss, I've heard you give that speech so many times, and I've heard you rehearse it so often, I could give it in my sleep."

"What size suit do you wear?", the economist inquired.

"A 42 long."

"Pull over at the next gas station, and we will exchange clothes."

They did it, and they proceeded on to Washington to a press conference. Dan Rather, Ted Koppel, Barbara Walters, and all the famed press were there. The chauffeur fooled them all. Then they rolled on to a packed JFK Stadium, where he delivered an eloquent forty-five-minute speech. He was all set to get off the stage when a hand went up in Section 13, Row 16, Seat 2. It was Doctor Milton Friedman, former chief economist to three past presidents.

"Sir," he asked, "based on the current political problems in the Kremlin, the falling price of the dollar in relationship to all the other currencies, and then in conjunction with the falling price of oil, what do you think the price of the Japanese yen will be between now and 2003?"

"Dr. Friedman," replied the speaker, "that's the dumbest question I've ever heard. To show you just how dumb it is, I'm going to let my chauffeur answer it."

❦❦❦

Being an economist is a great way to make a living because you can go your entire career without having to be right even once.

If you lay all economists end to end you could not reach a conclusion.

Economists have predicted seven of the last three recessions.

❦❦❦

Harry Truman, when he was president of the U.S.A., said, "Give me a one-armed economist because, every time I hear them say something, they say, 'but on the other hand.' I'm tired of the whole run of people that tell you tomorrow will be the end of the world. That's an easy prediction to make because, when it doesn't happen, no one is mad at them."

One of his economic advisors admitted that, "an economist is someone who studied numbers but didn't have the personality to be an accountant."

❦❦❦

Here is another genie joke, and the genie is still laughing:

A man was sitting alone in his office one evening when a genie popped out of an ashtray. The genie asked, "What will your third wish be?"

"Huh?", exclaimed the surprised guy. "How can I get a third wish before a first or second wish?"

"You have had two wishes already," the genie explained, "but your second wish was for me to put everything back the way it was before you made your first wish. Therefore you remember nothing, because everything is as it was prior to your first wishes. You have one wish left."

"I don't believe this, but what the heck, I wish I were irresistible to women."

"Funny," said the genie. "That was your first wish too."

❦❦❦

"There are no atheists in fox holes," according to an old saw.

One self-proclaimed atheist was enjoying his day fishing quietly on the Loch when, suddenly, his boat was attacked by the Loch Ness monster. With one easy flip, the beast tossed him and his boat high into the air. As the man sailed head over heels in the air, he saw the monster's open mouth, ready to swallow him. He cried out, "Oh my God, please help me!"

At once, the ferocious attack scene was frozen in place. As the atheist hung in mid-air, a powerful voice came out of the clouds, "I thought you didn't believe in me."

"Dear God, give me a break," the man pleaded. "Two minutes ago, I didn't believe in the Loch Ness monster either."

❦❦❦

In the beginning, God created the mule and told him, "As a mule you will work from dawn to dusk carrying heavy loads on your back. You will eat grass and lack intelligence. You will live fifty years." The mule pleaded, "To live like this for fifty years is too much. Give me only twenty years."

And it was so!

Then God created the dog. "You will hold vigilance over the dwellings of man, to whom you will be his most loyal companion. You will eat scraps from his table and live for twenty-five years." The dog responded, "Lord, to live as a dog like that is too much. Please, no more than ten years."

And it was so!

God then created the monkey. "You are monkey. You will swing from tree to tree, acting like an idiot. You will live for twenty years." "Oh no, Lord," the monkey cried, "To live twenty years as the clown of the world is too much. Please Lord, give me no more than ten years."

And it was so!

Finally God created Man. "You are Man, an intelligent being, the only rational one to walk on Earth. You will have mastery over the creatures of the world. You will dominate the earth and live for twenty years." The man responded, "Lord, to be Man for only twenty years is too little. Please, Lord, give me the twenty years the mule refused, the fifteen years the dog rejected, and the ten years the monkey didn't want."

And it was so!

So God made Man to live twenty years as a man, then marry and live twenty years carrying heavy loads on his back. Then, he would have children and live fifteen years as a dog, guarding his home and eating leftovers after the children have emptied the pantry. Then, in his old age, he would live ten years as a monkey, acting like an idiot to amuse his grandchildren.

And it was so!

❦❦❦

A minister, a priest, and a rabbi were considering the beginning of life.

The minister claimed, "Life begins when the heart begins to beat."

The priest stated, "Life begins at the moment of conception."

The rabbi commented, "No, life begins when the kids move out and the dog dies."

❦❦❦

Diana Fox contributed the following story. She is the young lady who drew the cartoons in this book. She wrote: Here is a little dry humor. This is one of the funniest things I've heard in a long time. I think this guy should have been promoted, not fired. This is a true story from the

WordPerfect help line, and it was transcribed from a recording monitoring the customer-care department. The help desk employee was fired, but he is currently challenging the WordPerfect organization for termination without cause. The actual dialogue follows (Now I know why they record these conversations.):

"Ridge Hall computer assistance, may I help you?"

"Yes, well, I'm having trouble with WordPerfect."

"What sort of trouble?"

"Well I was just typing along and all of a sudden the words went away."

"Went away?"

"They disappeared."

"Hmm. So what does your screen look like now?"

"Nothing."

"Nothing?"

"It's blank; It won't accept anything when I type."

"Are you still in WordPerfect, or did you get out?"

"How do I tell?"

"Can you see a C: prompt on the screen?"

"What's a sea-prompt?"

"Never mind, can you move your cursor around the screen?"

"There isn't any cursor. I told you; it won't accept anything when I type."

"Does your monitor have a power indicator?"

"What's a monitor?"

"It's the thing with the screen that looks like a TV. Does it have a little light that tells you when it is on?"

"I don't know."

"Well, then, look on the back of the monitor and find where the power cord goes into it. "Can you see that?"

"Yes, I think so."

"Great, now follow the cord to the plug and tell me if it is plugged into the wall."

"Yes, it is."

"When you were behind the monitor, did you notice that there were two cables plugged into the back of it, not just one?"

"No."

"Well, there are. I need you to look back there again and find the other cable."

"Okay, here it is."

"Follow it for me, and tell me if it's securely into the back of your computer."

"I can't reach."

"Uh huh. Well, can you see if it is?"

"No."

"Even if you maybe put your knee on something and lean way over?"

"Oh, it's not because I don't have the right angle. It's because it's dark."

"Dark?"

"Yes, the office light is off, and the only light is coming in from the window."

"Well, turn on the office light, then."

"I can't."

"No? Why not?"

"Because there's a power failure."

"A power ... a power failure? Aha, we've got it licked now. Do you still have the boxes and packing stuff your computer came in?"

"Yes, I keep them in the closet."

"Good. Go get them, and unplug your system and pack it up just like it was when you got it. Then take it back to the store you bought it from."

"Really, is it that bad?"

"Yes, I'm afraid it is."

"Well, all right, then, I suppose. What do I tell them?"

"Tell them you're too freaking stupid to own a computer."

❧❧❧

Ronald McKinley sent the following story about a new kind of law:

It seems that Johnny Cochrane was duck hunting recently. He attempted to cross a fence into a field to retrieve a duck he had shot. A farmer suddenly drove up in his truck, jumped out, and asked Cochrane what he was doing on his property.

"Retrieving this duck that I just shot," he replied.

The farmer stated, "It's on my side of the fence, so now it's mine."

Cochrane then asked the farmer if he recognized who he was talking to.

"No," replied the farmer, "I don't know, and I don't care."

"Does the name O. J. Simpson mean anything to you?"

"Yup," said the farmer, "I seen him on TV in that court case."

"I'm Johnny Cochrane from Los Angeles," came the reply. "I'm the lawyer that got O. J. Simpson off. I'm the reason he is a free man today. If you don't let me get that duck, I will sue you on the grounds of racial prejudice. I'll take your farm, your truck, and everything else you own. I'll leave you penniless on the street."

"Well," said the farmer, we ain't in Los Angeles. Here in the country, we go by the three kicks law."

"Never heard of it," stated Cochrane.

The farmer explained. "I get to kick you three times. Then, if you get back up on your feet and you are able to kick me back three times, the duck is yours."

Cochrane, always looking for a challenge to show his superiority, thought this over. He had grown up in a tough neighborhood. He figured he could take on and easily outdo this old farmer. "Okay," said Cochrane, "Fair enough."

"So, right off, the old farmer kicked Johnny violently in the groin. As the lawyer doubled over, the farmer kicked him in the face. Then, when Cochrane hit the ground, the farmer kicked him hard in the side, breaking several ribs. After several long moments and some failed attempts, Cochrane slowly made it back to his feet. Through clenched teeth, he says, "All right, now it's my turn."

The farmer smiled and said, "Naw, to hell with it. You can have the duck."

❦❦❦

When I started writing about humor, I pointed out to my wife that a large number of speakers and writers claimed that if you laugh enough you would never need visit a doctor. My wife quipped, "Yeah, they could just die laughing."

One day, I told my wife, "I think I'm becoming a ham."

She replied, "Oh no, you can cure a ham."

❦❦❦

A friend of mine, Larry Darling, wrote and published a book called *Entrepreneurism: Now it's Your Turn*. Larry has been an entrepreneur all his life. He started and successfully ran about twenty different businesses in his long career. He has been around for a long time. That is not to say that Larry is old, but he ain't no spring chicken. Larry is a very suave gentleman. He is from the old school, which means that he likes to be gallant with the fairer sex. One day, Larry was sitting on a crowded bus, reading his book. He looked up and saw a gorgeous girl in a tight red dress standing right in front of him. Chivalrously, Larry said, "I know I'm older than you but I would be most pleased if you would take my seat."

She declined sweetly. In a moment, the bus came to an abrupt screeching halt. All those standing were thrown forward into a heap. When they disentangled, Larry again asked, "Young lady, if you won't take my seat, why don't you sit on my lap to decongest the crowd?"

She did just that. The bus went on its bumpy way for a while. Then Larry tapped her on the shoulder and said, "Young lady. I'm afraid you'll have to stand up again. I'm not as old as I thought I was."

❧❧❧

Recently, there has been considerable debate about the nationality of Adam and Eve. Some anthropologists held a convention to determine the question of nationality.

The British anthropologist was the first to speak. He said, "But naturally, gentlemen, they are British. In what other culture would a gentleman share his only apple with a lady?"

The French anthropologist got up next and replied, "No, mon ami, they are French. In what other culture would a lady share the love of a gentleman for only an apple?"

Finally, the Russian got up and said, "You are both wrong. They are Russian. Look at them. They are naked. They have only one apple between them, and they have been convinced that they are in paradise."

❧❧❧

It's difficult to think of Russians in Russia with a sense of humor. However, though it may be a little different, the Russians do exhibit a joy of the use of humor, as shown in the following anecdote. It was told by a Russian diplomat to explain the Russian economy. "Two fellows were walking along the edge of a cliff. One of them fell off. The companion waited to hear a thud. When he didn't hear a thud, he leaned over and shouted, "Are you all right down there?"

"Yeah, I'm all right," came the reply.

"Anything broken?"

"No, nothing's broken."

"Well, come on back up."

"I can't. I'm still falling."

> *Any time you wake up in the morning*
> *and there's not a chalk outline around your body,*
> *you are truly blessed.*

Ralph Waldo Emerson on success and humor!

Success is to laugh often and much; to win the respect of intelligent people and the affection of children; to earn the appreciation of honest critics and to endure the betrayal of false friends: to appreciate beauty, to find the best in others; to leave the world a bit better, whether by a healthy child, a garden patch, or a redeemed social condition; to know even one life has breathed easier because you have lived. This is to have succeeded.

It requires a great deal of boldness and a great deal of caution to make a great fortune, and when you have got it, it requires ten times as much wit to keep it.

These thoughts may be somewhat heavy for a book on humor, but Emerson clearly believed in the use of humor to lighten the load in daily living. Surely we can tolerate a little philosophy at this point from a great thinker.

Angels can fly because they take themselves lightly.

In his book, *Man's Search for Meaning*, Victor Frankl said, "Everything can be taken from a man but one thing: the last of the human freedoms, to choose one's attitude in a given set of circumstances, to choose one's own way."

☞☞☞

Einstein stated:
"The thinking that has got me this far has created some problems that this thinking can't solve."

There is an interesting story told about Albert Einstein. This is the story as told by a speaker during a convention of life insurance agents.

It seems that Einstein had a nephew who was a professor at MIT. He was visiting his famous uncle and noted that his uncle was in an extra-special mood. He commented to his uncle, "Uncle Al, I have never seen you so relaxed and happy."

"I've just come back from a most enjoyable trip to the West Coast," responded Einstein. "On the plane ride back, I sat next to Niels Bohr, and his IQ must be at least 175. We spent the entire trip discussing the internal structure of the atom. It was a delightful conversation, and the time just seemed to pass so quickly. The next time he ran into his uncle, Einstein looked even more pleased and relaxed than on the previous occasion. He said, "Uncle Al, you look marvelous."

"I just came back from a conference in Europe and on the plane ride home I sat next to Werner Heisenberg. We had a most wonderful discussion about his theories of quantum mechanics. This man is a true genius. His IQ must be over 180."

Unfortunately, the next time the professor saw his uncle, he didn't look so good. He said, "Uncle Al, what's the problem? You don't look too well."

"Well, I just returned from a trip to Stanford University, and I got stuck next to a moron. His IQ couldn't have been more than 60."

"So what did you discuss?"

"We discussed the difference between term and whole life."

(A similar story has been related elsewhere. I tell it again to demonstrate how you can use an old story in a new way to fit the situation.)

There is not one shred of evidence to support the belief that life is serious. Lighten up!

Aerobics is a good example of taking life too seriously! I'm not a couch potato, but I can't get serious about aerobics. The definition of aerobics that I like is stated, "Any of a number of languages spoken by Islamic people."

It's scary to think that the person who thought up aerobics may now be thinking up something else. I tried that stuff for almost an hour, one time, and it didn't work.

Garfield, the philosopher cat, asked: "Who thought up aerobics, and were they properly punished?"

When I was a teenager on the farm, I wanted a set of barbells just like my friend had. I told my father about it, and he scoffed at me. "Pumping weights is like loading a truck that's not there. Come outside and pitch some hay. We'll put that energy to good use."

🐾🐾🐾

Bankers!

A drunk wandered into a graveyard and read a grave stone inscription, "Here lies a banker and an honest man."

He observed to another inebriated friend, "Hey, it's getting so crowded now that they are burying two people in one grave."

🐾🐾🐾

When a bank in the U.S.A. failed recently, one creditor observed, "I have learned that the difference between a pigeon and a director of a failed bank is the pigeon can still make a small deposit on a Mercedes."

🐾🐾🐾

An elderly gentleman drove up to a small bank in New York in his Rolls Royce. The bank president happened to be looking out the window and saw the elderly gentleman drive up. He rushed out to meet him. The distinguished gentleman stated that he wanted to borrow $1,000 for thirty days. He would leave his Rolls Royce as collateral for the loan. It was apparent that the old gent didn't need the money, but the bank president didn't want to offend him, so he loaned the money for thirty days and took the car as collateral. The bank president took the keys to the car, parked it in his personal garage, and made sure it was clean and well taken care of. Thirty days later, the elderly gentleman returned with the $1,000 plus $10 interest. He got the keys to his Rolls and was about to walk out the front door. The bank president couldn't stand it any longer, so he asked, "I just don't understand it. Why did you do this?"

The elderly gentleman explained with a wry smile, "Well, I was going to Europe for thirty days. If I parked it anywhere else in Manhattan, it would cost $30 a day. This way, it cost only $10 for the entire thirty days."

It pays to be aware of your options!

Inflation means that your money won't buy as much as when you didn't have any!

Try to please everybody and what happens?

An old man and his grandson were going on a journey with their donkey. When they started out, the young lad was sitting on the donkey. The old man took the lead rope and started to walk. Before they got very far, people began to notice and to criticize, "Look at the boy riding and that old man is walking."

So they stopped, the young boy got down, and the old man got up, and they continued on their way. They did not get very far before people were saying, "Look at that man riding while that poor child has to walk."

They stopped and both of them got on the donkey, and they continued their journey. They didn't get very far before all the people were saying, "Look at that poor little donkey having to carry two people."

So they stopped, got off, and started to carry the poor little donkey. As they walked, they reached a wobbly bridge. While crossing it, they slipped and dropped the donkey in the river, and it drowned. The old man looked at his grandson and said, "We learned a valuable lesson today. If you listen to all the people you will lose your ass."

❧❧❧

Nido Qubein could not speak English when he came to America. He was always amazed by the way we use words. For example, one day he looked at the label on a shirt collar, which said, "Skrink resistant." He asked a saleslady, "What does that mean? It either shrinks or it doesn't." Her answer was classic: "Sir, that means the garment will shrink, but it doesn't want to."

Do you hear voices?

One day, a man was shaving in his bathroom when he heard a voice behind him. It seemed to be coming from everywhere and yet nowhere. He thought he was alone in the apartment. The voice said, "Close out all your savings, margin your stocks, put your money in a bag, and go to Las Vegas." The guy could not believe it. He wondered if someone was playing a joke on him, so he went back to shaving.

But the voice came again, "Close out all of your savings, margin your stocks, put the money in a bag, and go to Vegas."

Confused, the guy started rushing around his apartment, looking for the source of the message. When he got to the living room, the voice said, "I'm not going to say it again."

Well, the guy thought it was kind of crazy, but he decided to do it anyway. He closed his savings accounts, margined his stocks, put all the money in a gym bag, and got on a bus for Las Vegas. As he got off the bus, the voice said, "Caesar's Palace."

So, looking neither left nor right, he headed to Caesar's Palace. He entered the door; the voice stated, "Blackjack."

So he walked to the nearest blackjack table. The voice said, "Bet it all, one hand."

He advised the dealer, "I want to bet it all on one hand."

The dealer replied, "I'm sorry, but we can't accept that large a bet."

The voice instructed, "Tell him to ask the manager."

So the guy requested, "Would you ask the manager?"

The manager gave his okay, so the dealer dealt the hand.

The dealer was showing an eight. The bettor had a ten and a three. The instructor said, "Hit."

Well, he had figured that out already, so he said, "Hit me."

He got a four and now he had 17. At this point, he got really anxious. Seventeen is not a great hand, especially with the dealer showing an eight. The instructional voice said, "Hit."

As sweat started to show on his brow, the guy choked out, "Hit."

The dealer dealt a three. Now he had 20. Relief flooded over him, and he was starting to congratulate himself because his 20 would almost certainly beat what looked like the dealer's 18. And then the voice said, "Hit."

The guy stopped breathing, and, in a voice he could hardly recognize, he blurted out, "Hit me."

The dealer turned over the card. It was an ace!

And the voice exclaimed, "Unbelievable!"

❦❦❦

How about the fellow who went to Las Vegas and decided to make mental bets only. He went to the roulette table and placed a mental bet. He went to the blackjack table and placed a mental bet. He did this for three days. Then guess what happened? "He lost his mind!"

❦❦❦

Todd Skinner and his partner free-climbed the face of a rock in Yosemite. Free-climbing is climbing without the use of conventional equipment. They were on the face of this rock for six days and six nights. Todd was asked the question, "How did you sleep at night?"

Todd replied, "We slept like babies. We woke up every two hours and cried."

❦❦❦

According to some psychologists, people can be classified into four categories according to behavioral styles. The categories are: the *Director*, the *Relater*, the *Socializer*, and the *Thinker*.

To illustrate the difference, Tony Allessandra, Ph.D., likes to relate the following story: "Many years ago, in the days of Louis XIV, four noblemen were accused of a very serious crime. They were put on trial, and, although they protested their innocence vehemently, they were convicted and sentenced to death by guillotine. On the fateful day of execution, a special guillotine was constructed so that all four could be beheaded simultaneously. The four noblemen—one a *Director*, one a *Relater*, one a *Socializer*, and one a *Thinker*, were placed in position for the execution.

Upon receiving word from Louis XIV, the executioner swung his axe, cut the rope, and the blade descended rapidly toward the necks of the noblemen. Just as the blades touched their necks, the mechanism jammed. Louis XIV saw this as a sign from above that the noblemen were truly innocent, as they had protested during the trial. He set them free.

As they were freed, each nobleman expressed his appreciation in different ways, very much according to his own individual style. The first one freed was the *Director*. As he got up from the guillotine, he looked at everyone and said, "I told you I was innocent. Now next time maybe you will listen to me when I tell you something. And Louis, let me tell you something: I'm suing!"

The second person freed was the *Relater*. He went right up to the executioner and said, "I know this wasn't your fault. I'm not going to hold it against you. Would you come over for dinner on Sunday?"

The third one freed was the *Socializer*. He jumped up, looked at everyone and said, "Let's party!"

The last one released was the *Thinker*. As he was getting up, he looked up at the guillotine and said, "I think I see the problem."

I learn from my mistakes.
I have found that I can make the same mistake
with much greater ease the second time around!

A well-known speaker was asked to give a lecture to a young people's church group on the subject of marriage. His wife heard that he was going to give the lecture, and she asked, "What are you going to be talking about?" Having just finished talking to a friend about sailing, and knowing that he was not an expert on marriage, he answered with the first thing that popped into his mind: "It's a class on sailing."

His wife, Lora, gave him a quizzical look but went on her way without another word. She had a previous commitment. Thus, she could not attend his lecture. He thought it was just as well because his wife might be somewhat skeptical about his qualification as an authority on marriage.

The evening came and went, and the class went very well. In fact, it went so well that several of the engaged couples came up to Lora at church the following Sunday and remarked about how excellent the class had been. They told her how wonderfully knowledgeable her husband was.

Lora was somewhat confused, and she blurted out, "I don't get it. He's only done it twice in his life. The first time he got sick, and the second time his hat blew off."

❦❦❦

One speaker asked his audience, "Do you always make good choices?" Then he related a story about an elderly clergyman who was walking down the street when he saw one of his friends on his knees on the front lawn. The clergyman asked, "What are you looking for? Maybe I can help you find it."

The old chap looked up at the minister and said, "Well, I lost my house keys. I can't find my house keys."

The minister said, "Well, tell me where you lost them, and I'll help you find them."

The old boy replied, "I lost them in the house."

The minister chuckled at that and asked, "Well, then, why are you looking for them out here?"

The somewhat confused parishioner replied, "There's more light out here!" (I warned you that I like corny jokes.)

❦❦❦

Another speaker explained his misspent youth (and that of his buddies), being in constant trouble with the authorities: "We had a terrible habit of finding things before they were lost."

He said that he adored his mother-in-law: "I love to buy her presents. She is always so appreciative. One time I bought her a beautiful chair, but my wife wouldn't let me plug it in." (Take your time; you'll get it.)

❦❦❦

There is humor in adversity!

Policemen can be sources of humor. This story illustrates that police officers have a human side, after all. An Indiana police officer responded to the scene of a barricaded suspect. That is a situation where an armed suspect barricades himself in his home, usually after having committed some crime, and he refuses to come out. This officer responded at a time before SWAT techniques of containment, evacuation, and fire control were developed. He decided he would be a hero and get the guy out by himself. He made two rookie mistakes, considering that you should never decide in advance to be a hero, and, secondly, you should work as a team in any crisis situation. Well, this officer took a tear-gas grenade in one hand, and his service revolver in the other hand. He approached the door where the suspect was barricaded. Being human, the adrenaline started to work. In other words, he was nervous, and sometimes that can crowd out critical thinking. Such was the case with this very human cop.

He pulled the pin from the tear-gas grenade, John Wayne style, with his teeth, kicked the door open, and tossed his revolver into the room with the suspect. When his human brain caught up with what he had done, he realized that, not only had he disarmed himself, but he was about to tear gas himself.

He glanced inside and saw that the suspect had committed suicide, probably long before his arrival on the scene. He quietly picked up his gun and holstered it. He found the grenade pin, put it back in place, and didn't tell a soul about this sequence of events. There is a statute of limitations on stupidity. The officer waited for it to run out before he ever told the story, even to another cop.

☙☙☙

Many people have heard the motivational speaker Zig Ziglar. His passion is motivating people. He says, "Let's motivate them—get them going."

One of his buddies replied, "Zig, if a guy is going in the wrong direction, and if you motivate him, he will get to disaster quicker. If the guy is an idiot, you have a motivated idiot."

However, Zig is the master and some of his stuff is classic. We are but students. Zig has been known to say, "Money isn't everything, but it ranks right up there with oxygen."

Zig says his dentist told him, "Only floss the teeth you want to keep. You can forget the others."

☙☙☙

Motivational speakers make me hungry for more!

Have you heard about the ninety-one-year-old lady who recently started walking for her health? Her son reported that she was walking five miles a day. Now she is ninety-three years-old and nobody knows where she is. Get your in-laws out walking. It could solve a lot of problems.

❦❦❦

Perhaps, a good exercise for some in-laws would be shoveling snow, especially if they live in Ottawa. A friend of my brother's sent him a copy of the diary of a new resident's snow-shoveling experience. It read:

December 8, 6:00 p.m.: It started to snow. The first snow of the season, and the wife and I took our cocktails and sat by the window for hours, watching the huge soft flakes float down from Heaven. It looked like a Grandma Moses print. So romantic, we felt like newlyweds again. I love snow!

December 9: We awoke to a beautiful blanket of crystal white snow covering every inch of the landscape. What a fantastic sight! Can there be a more lovely place in the whole world? Moving here was the best idea I've ever had. Shoveled for the first time in years, and I felt like a boy again. I did both the sidewalks and the driveway. This afternoon a snowplow came along and closed in the driveway, so I had to shovel again. What a perfect life!

December 12: The sun has melted all our lovely snow. Such a disappointment! My neighbor tells me not to worry. We will definitely have a white Christmas. No snow on Christmas would be awful. Bob says we'll have so much snow by the end of winter that I'll never want to see snow again. I don't think that's possible. I'm glad Bob is our neighbor.

December 14: Snow, lovely snow—eight inches last night. The temperature dropped to minus 20. The cold makes everything sparkle so. The wind took my breath away, but I warmed up shoveling the driveway, and sidewalks. This is the life! The snowplow came back this afternoon and buried everything again. I didn't realize I would have to do quite this much shoveling, but I'll certainly get back in shape this way. I wish I wouldn't huff and puff so much.

December 15: Twenty inches of snow forecast. I sold my van and bought a 4x4 Blazer. I bought snow tires for my wife's car and two extra shovels. We stocked the freezer. The wife wants a wood stove in case the electricity goes out. I think that's silly. After all, we are not in Alaska, you know.

December 16: Ice storm this morning. I fell on my butt on the ice in the driveway while putting down salt. It hurt like hell. The wife laughed for an hour, which I think was very cruel.

December 17: Still way below zero. The electricity was off for five hours. I had to pile the blankets on to stay warm. There's nothing to do but stare at the wife and try not to irritate her. I guess I should have bought a wood stove, but I won't admit that to her. Lord, I hate it when she's right. I can't believe I'm freezing to death in my own living room.

December 20: Electricity is back on, but we had another fourteen inches of the damned stuff. More shoveling! Took all day. Darned snowplow; came by twice. I tried to find a neighbor kid to help shovel. They all said they were too busy playing hockey. I think they are lying. I called the hardware to see about buying a snow blower, and they're out. They said there might be another shipment in March. I think they're lying! Bob says I have to shovel or the city will have it done, and bill me. I think he's lying.

December 22: Bob was right about a white Christmas because another thirteen inches of the white shit fell today. It's so damned cold it probably won't melt until August. It took forty-five minutes to get dressed to go out to shovel, and then I had to piss. By the time I got undressed, pissed, and dressed again, I was too tired to shovel. I tried to hire Bob, who has a plow on his truck, for the rest of the winter. He says he is too busy. I think the butthole is lying.

December 23: Only two inches of snow fell today, and it warmed up to zero. The wife wanted me to decorate the front of the house this morning. What is she, nuts? Why didn't she tell me to do that a month ago? She says she did, but I think she is lying.

December 23: Six inches. The snow was packed so hard, by the snowplow, I broke the shovel. I thought I was having a heart attack. If I ever catch the son of a bitch that drives that snowplow, I'll drag him through the snow by his balls. I know he hides around the corner and waits for me to finish shoveling, and then he comes down the street and throws snow over where I've been. Tonight the wife wanted me to sing Christmas carols with her, and open our presents, but I was too busy watching for the damned snowplow.

December 25: Merry Christmas! Twenty inches more of the *!x#d*!#!x1* slop tonight. Snowed in! The idea of shoveling makes my blood boil. Lord, I hate the snow! The snowplow driver came by asking for a donation, and I hit him over the head with my snow shovel. The wife says I have a bad attitude. I think she's an idiot. If I have to watch *It's a Wonderful Life* one more time, I'm going to kill her.

December 26: Still snowed in! Why the hell did I ever move here? It was all her idea. She's really getting on my nerves.

December 27: Temperature dropped to minus 30, and the pipes froze.

December 28: Warmed up to above minus 50. We're still snowed in. The bitch is driving me crazy!!!

December 29: Ten more inches. Bob says I have to shovel the roof or it could cave in. That's the silliest thing I ever heard. How dumb does he think I am?

December 30: Roof caved in. The snowplow driver is suing me for a million bucks. The wife went home to her mother. Nine inches predicted.

December 31: Set fire to what's left of the house. No more shoveling!

January 8: I feel so good. I just love those little white pills they keep giving me. Why am I tied to the bed?

A million dollars doesn't always bring happiness! A person, with $10 million, is no happier than another person, who has only $9 million.

My friends, Al and Beverlie Johnson, gave me a list of strange things they found in church bulletins:

- Announcement for a national Prayer and Fasting conference: "The cost for attending includes meals."

- Ladies don't forget the rummage sale. It's a chance to get rid of all those things not worth keeping around the house. Don't forget your husbands.
- The sermon this morning: "Jesus Walks on Water!" The sermon this evening: "Looking for Jesus!"
- Next Thursday, there will be tryouts for the choir. They need all the help they can get.
- Don't let worry kill you. Let the church help.
- At the evening service tonight, the sermon topic will be "What is Hell?" Come early and listen to our choir practice.
- For those who have children, and don't know it, there is a nursery downstairs.
- The church will host an evening of fine dining, superb entertainment, and gracious hostility.
- Low self-esteem group will meet Thursday morning, at 10. Please use the back door.
- The eighth-graders will be presenting Shakespeare's *Hamlet* in the church basement, Friday at 7 p.m. The congregation is invited to attend this tragedy.
- The associate minister unveiled the church's new tithing campaign slogan last Sunday: "I Upped My Pledge—Up Yours."

ʊʊʊ

After a speaker finished his program in Spokane, Washington, he realized he had over five hours before his plane left. He decided to go golfing—his favorite hobby. When he was flying into Spokane, he had noticed a golf course near the airport. So out he went, rented some clubs, and was all set to go, all by himself, with just enough time to make it. He ran to the first tee and was all set to tee off when an eighty-five-year-old man approached and asked to play along. He stated, "I'm all by myself too."

The speaker thought, "Oh no! I'm going to miss my flight." However, to say no would be disrespectful, so he said, "sure, no problem." John introduced himself to the older gent and learned that his name was Ernie. Well, the old boy walked faster than did John. He hit the ball straighter, too. He was a pure joy to golf with. Ernie gave John a quote for every hole. On the first hole, he said, "Mark Twain said, 'Age is a matter of mind. If you don't mind, it doesn't matter'."

At the second hole, he said, "John, your face, after age forty, is your own fault."

On the fourteenth fairway, there was an enormous pine tree about fifty yards in front of John's ball. He could not cut around it, and he didn't know if he could hit the ball over the tree. In his deliberations, he was taking too much time. The old boy, Ernie, walked over and said," Hit the ball John; you haven't got all day."

John replied, "Sorry, Ernie, but I haven't seen a tree that tall on a golf course. I don't know if I could hit the ball over it."

Ernie chuckled and said, "Let me give you a secret, John. When I was your age, I could hit the ball over that tree."

So, trusting this advice, John took out his three iron and made a perfect swing. It had no chance of clearing the tree! It drilled the tree three-quarters of the way up, and the ball bounced back toward them. John looked at Ernie, and the old boy said, "You didn't let me finish. When I was your age that tree was only twenty feet tall."

❦❦❦

Humor is not just telling jokes! Humor comes in many forms. Among other things, it may be a series of one-liners, as we hear from many comedians. Sometimes, a speaker or author may use a story or anecdote to set up the punch line. Some of the best humor develops when the listener does not anticipate a funny punch line. Another way to do this is to develop a concept wherein the use of humor is not necessary. The humorous finish merely illustrates your point, concept, or theme. A funny punch line is an added benefit or bonus that makes your point memorable.

Comedians are usually trying to entertain an audience rather than to educate it. Many have found one-liners most effective. Bob Newhart and Bill Cosby are adept at telling stories to set up a humorous ending. Both can also deliver one-liners effectively. Bob Hope is (and George Burns was) a master of one-liners. Their timing is often mentioned when people discuss their brand of humor.

❦❦❦

Here are some one-liners from Dottie Waters book, *What to Say, When You're Dying on the Platform:*

> "Wit is the sudden marriage of ideas, which before their union were not perceived to have any relationship." ~ *Mark Twain*

If your humor bombs, say:

> "That was a joke designed to get a silent laugh, and it worked perfectly." ~ *Roger Langley*

Look at one person in your audience and say:

> "That's the last time I'm going to use *your* material." ~ *Unknown*

> "Well, Mom liked it!"

> "When my wife heard that joke, she said, 'You'll never get a laugh.' She was right!" ~ *Ken Blanchard*

Some salespeople are so lazy that they step into a revolving door and wait.

One fellow I heard speak said, "I'm dyslexic and I'm dysphagic. And yes, you're right, I can't spell either of them."

❧❧❧

Carole Jeffries sent some sayings that should be on buttons:

- Are those your eyeballs? I found them in my cleavage.
- I'm not your type. I'm not inflatable.
- I'm trying to imagine you with a personality.
- Don't worry, I forgot your name too!
- Well, this day was a total waste of makeup.
- Make yourself at home. Clean my kitchen.
- Don't bother me. I'm living happily ever after.
- Do I look like a freakin' people person?
- I started out with nothing, and I still have most of it left.

- An office cubicle is a padded cell without a door.
- I thought I wanted a career; turns out I just wanted paychecks.
- I'm just working here until a good fast-food job opens up.
- I pretend to work. They pretend to pay me.
- Diamonds are just lumps of coal that worked a little harder.
- You, off my planet.
- Errors have been made. Others will be blamed.
- I'm not crazy. I've been in a bad mood for thirty years.
- Allow me to introduce my selves.
- Sarcasm is one more service we offer.
- Do they ever shut up on your planet?
- I can't remember if I'm the good twin or the evil one.
- How many times do I flush before you go away?
- I just want revenge. Is that so wrong?
- You say I'm a bitch like it's a bad thing.
- Can I trade this job for what's behind door #2?
- Ah, chaos, panic, and disorder; my work is done here.
- Earth is full. Go home!
- How do I set a laser printer to stun.
- I'm not tense, just terribly, terribly alert.
- Free advice is worth the price.
- He is the type of guy a bartender asks to leave so they can start happy hour.

🐝🐝🐝

Do you enjoy newspaper headlines? Check out the following:

- Grandmother of eight makes hole in one.
- Police begin campaign to run down jaywalkers.
- Two convicts evade noose—jury hung.
- Milk drinkers are turning to powder.
- Safety experts say school bus passengers should be belted.
- Queen Mary is having her bottom scraped.
- Prostitutes appeal to the Pope.
- Squad helps dog bite victim.
- Lawmen from Mexico barbecue guests.
- Minors refuse to work after death.
- Two Soviet ships collide—one dies.
- Two sisters reunite after eighteen years at checkout counter.

🐝🐝🐝

Question on an exam paper: "What do you think is the greatest danger facing our country today—ignorance or apathy?"

One student answered, "I don't know and I don't care."

❦❦❦

There is an anecdote about an individual who was sitting on the deck of the *Titanic*. While the band was playing "Nearer My God to Thee," he was sitting in his bathrobe, next to a bulkhead, reading a novel by flashlight. Someone asked him, "How come you're so cool, calm, and collected? All the rest of us are in a tizzy." The guy took off his glasses, folded down the corner of a page so he would not lose his place, and calmly replied, "Why should I worry; it's not my boat."

Cartoon humor:

Two Ubangi's were sitting by the fire. One turned to the other and said, "Instead of hunting tonight, why don't we call our insurance agent and tell him we want to increase our coverage? When he comes we will eat him." (You can change this one by inserting, "... call a speaker to an audition" or, "... call an author to bring some of his books.")

Another cartoon:

The general is standing on the field of battle, sword in hand. The salesman behind him wants to demonstrate a machine gun. The caption reads: "I can't be bothered with a pesky salesman. I've got a battle to fight."

❦❦❦

A tiger hunter had been stocking a Bengal tiger for six weeks without success. Upon returning from a hard day in the jungle, he came around a corner and stood facing a 1,300-pound Bengal tiger. It had not eaten for several weeks. Quickly dropping to one knee, the hunter pulled the rifle to his shoulder. Just as the tiger leapt, the hunter fired off a round. Both the hunter and the tiger missed, and both ran away. The hunter raced down the trail to his camp. That night, about two o'clock in the morning, he awoke from his tossing and turning, and he could not get back to sleep thinking about the near fatal meeting with the tiger. Taking his 303 rifle and a box of cartridges, the hunter went to a nearby clearing in the jungle. Just as the sun rose over his campsite, he started practising. He shot at fleas, gnats, butterflies, and any small target he could find. He fired from one knee, two knees, lying down, standing up, and sitting down. He practised short-range shots. As he paused to reload, he heard a noise in the distance. There was the sound of crashing, thumping, and banging. Taking his rifle, the hunter sneaked quietly through the underbrush. There in a clearing in the middle of the deepest darkest jungle, he witnessed an amazing event. There before his eyes was the tiger practising short leaps.

The moral of this story is clearly, you need to work on the small things.

🐾🐾🐾

There are many jokes about two people being confronted by a dangerous animal such as a lion or a bear. One of the pair starts putting on and lacing up his running shoes. His companion says, "Why are you tying your running shoes? You can't outrun a bear."

The first guy replies, "No, but I can outrun you."

Most people, judging by the laughter, consider this to be funny. It may be, except for one little error. If one person runs, and the other one plays dead, the animal, lion or bear, will go after the moving target. It's instinctive for animals to run down their prey. If I were part of that scenario, I would say, "Hey good idea, you take off, and I'll hide in these bushes."

Stranded in paradise:

Two businessmen were on a trip to Mexico when, suddenly, their plane went down. It crashed in the Gulf of Mexico, near a small deserted atol. The senior businessman stripped off his expensive three-piece Italian suit and went for a swim. After a refreshing fifteen minutes, he climbed a tree and cut down some pineapples and bananas and made a fruit salad. Then, he went back and did a little fishing, went for a stroll, relaxed in the sun, and then went for another swim. He was enjoying his moment of solitude.

The younger companion watched all of this for about an hour and a half. He grew very uptight and shouted at his friend, "What are you doing? We are in the middle of the Gulf of Mexico. We have got to get rescued. What are you doing? Resting and relaxing, that's all. We've got to do something to get rescued."

The older gentleman said, "Relax, my young friend, don't worry so much. Two years ago, when my business took off, I was so thankful that I gave $10,000 to the church. Last year, business was even better, and, to show my gratitude, I donated $25,000. This year has been the best one ever, financially. I plan to give even more than before and the church knows about it. Don't worry; they will find me."

❦❦❦

One newlywed was overheard talking to a bride-to-be. "Marriage is really a grind. You do the dishes, make the beds, do the laundry, and then, two weeks later, you have to do it all over again."

❦❦❦

Last year, I went golfing with some of my friends at one of the toughest courses in Alberta. This was a very difficult course. I lost twelve balls, five of them in ball washers. I stepped up to the tee on the first par three, over water. Why are par three's always over water? I did what I normally do. I put down an old ball. Then I heard a voice behind me, "Play a new ball."

I went back to my bag and took out the only Titleist I have. For some time now, I have had a deal with the company. They are paying me to not use their balls. Anyway, I put down my only new ball and stood back to look at my target. A voice said, "Take a practice swing."

So I took a practice swing. And the voice said, "Play the old ball."

❦❦❦

One of the members of CAPS (Canadian Association of Professional Speakers) presented himself to Brian Lee, one of the most successful speakers in the world. He stated, "I want to become the greatest speaker of all time."

Brian asked him, "Are you prepared to be ridiculed, ignored, and frustrated until you are over forty?"

"I am," replied the young man. "But tell me, what will happen after age forty?"

"You'll get used to it," Brian quipped.

When are people glad to be down and out?
After a bumpy plane ride.

When we landed in Windsor, Ontario, after a relatively short trip from Toronto, the plane was caught in what is known as a "cross wind." The plane came in hard, bounced on the runway, and came down again to glide smoothly toward the terminal. The pilot came on the speaker and said, "By now, you all know we have landed."

❧❧❧

On another trip, we flew from Calgary to Montreal, took on passengers, and headed for New York City. When we arrived, cloud and weather conditions made it impossible to land right away. We circled above the city for about an hour before returning to Montreal. The passengers disembarked and waited in a secured room for another hour. We had already cleared customs, so we could not leave this room.

During this period of forced enclosure, I was able to speak with the captain. I asked him what would happen if we were not able to land on our next attempt. The captain advised us that we had an alternate destination—Boston.

"Well, okay," I said, "But how about Bermuda, I haven't been there for a while."

He laughed and assured me that the alternate would have to be Boston. Finally, we were boarded once again, and we waited for takeoff. After nearly an hour, the captain came on the speaker and offered free drinks and nourishment. Then, he added, "I'm sure that most of you would prefer to be down here wishing you were up there, rather than up there wishing you were down here."

We agreed!

❧❧❧

On still another flight, there were a number of us going to the same convention. This usually makes for a somewhat rowdy group. The plane we were boarding came from Edmonton, and some of our associates were already seated. One of my northern acquaintances was a man by the name of "Jack." As I was stowing my carry-on, Jack called to me from several rows back: "Hi, Lyle."

I turned to him and said "Hi —."

I froze in mid-sentence. Everyone chuckled as I revised my greeting to "Hello, Jack."

❧❧❧

For all those men who are tired of male-bashing jokes, here are some comments that you may enjoy:

- What's worse than a male chauvinist pig? A woman who won't do what she is told.
- I married Miss Right. I just didn't know that her middle name was "Always."
- Scientists have discovered a food that diminishes a woman's sex drive by ninety percent. It's called "a wedding cake."
- Our last fight was my fault. My wife asked me, "What's on TV?" I answered, "Dust."
- Young son: "Is it true, Dad, that in some parts of Africa a man doesn't know his wife until he marries her?" Dad's reply: "That happens in every country, son."
- "Women will never be equal with men until they can walk down Main Street bald-headed with a beer gut and still think they are beautiful."

- Alternatively, there is a bumper sticker that claims, *"Women who want to be equal to men lack ambition."*

❧❧❧

Here are some appraisals reportedly used in the U.S. Army:

- Not the sharpest knife in the drawer.
- Got into the gene pool when the lifeguard wasn't watching.
- He's got a room temperature IQ.
- His photographic memory has the lens cap glued on.
- He's a primary candidate for natural de-selection.

- He's as bright as Alaska in December.
- One-celled organisms outscore him on IQ tests.
- He fell out of the family tree.
- He is so dense, light bends around him.
- If brains were taxed, he would get a rebate.
- Any more stupid, he'd need to be watered twice a week.
- If you stand close to him, you can hear the ocean.
- He's one neuron short of a synapse.
- It takes him an hour and a half to watch "60 Minutes."

❦❦❦

At Texas A & M University, they like to tell stories about their graduates. One of them heard that the police department needed recruits desperately. He went to the station and applied. The chief said, "You have just got to answer three questions and the job is yours.

Number one: "What is 1 and 1?"

The lad replied, "That's hard, Chief, but I got the answer: "11."

The old chief chuckled, "Well, I didn't say 1+1, so this boy's got it."

Two: "What two days of the week start with the letter T?"

"That's harder than the first question, Chief, but I think I've got it. It's today and tomorrow."

The chief smiled, "Well, that's not incorrect."

Last question: "Who killed Abraham Lincoln?"

"I don't rightly know that one, Chief. We never studied that at A&M."

"Well," said the chief, "you go home and study up on it and come back tomorrow. If you've got the right answer, you got the job."

When he got home, his wife asked, "How did you do on the test?"

"Well," he told her, "I must have done pretty good, they got me working on a murder case already."

❦❦❦

Do you know the difference between a Texas tale and a fairy tale? A fairy tale begins, "Once upon a time." A Texas tale begins, "Now listen up, 'cause you ain't gonna believe this." Now listen up:

Bubba Joe and Billy Jack are two Texas hunters. They live way out in the country. These two old boys went hunting and shot a deer, one day. They were dragging it back to their truck by the tail, making all kinds of noise, rattling bushes and stomping through the trees and huffing and puffing.

A local farmer happened by and saw what they were doing. He looked at those two old boys and said, "Bubba Joe and Billy Jack, God made a perfect set of handles for dragging that deer by—antlers."

Now the boys thought this was a good idea, so they walked around to the front of the deer and started dragging it by the horns. After about fifteen minutes, Bubba Joe turned to Billy Jack and said, "You know, this is a lot easier than dragging it by the tail."

And Billy Jack replied, "Yeah, but it's getting us further and further from the pickup truck."

🦆🦆🦆

Two other hunters went out duck hunting one morning. When they left home at 5:00 a.m., it was rather dark and cold.

Joe was a coffee drinker, and he took a thermos of coffee. Pedro didn't drink coffee, so he took a flask of gin to keep him warm. They sat waiting for several hours without seeing a duck. During this time, Joe finished his thermos of coffee, and Pedro polished off the flask of gin.

Suddenly, a lone duck flew by.

Excitedly, Joe, the coffee drinker, raised his shotgun to his shoulder and emptied both barrels. He missed! Pedro, the gin drinker, shot from the hip and brought the duck down with one shot.

Joe, the coffee drinker, exclaimed, "That's some pretty good shooting!"

Pedro, the gin drinker, slurred back, "Hell no-no, I-I should a got a least two or three from a flock that big."

🦆🦆🦆

Two hunters from south of the border flew to Saskatchewan to hunt elk for four days. They went over to the small local airport and found a pilot. "Sir, we would like to rent your plane and have you fly us into this lake on the chart."

The Canadian bush pilot explained, "I can't fly my plane onto that lake. It's too small."

One of the hunters said, "That's funny. We were here in this very hanger one year ago with another bush pilot, and he flew us onto that lake."

The pilot replied, "Well, if another pilot can do it, so can I."

He did it! He flew them onto the lake with no difficulty. One of the hunters instructed him, "Now, you get back here in four days."

Four days later, the pilot flew back to the lake, and there were the proud hunters standing on the dock. They had shot three elk, and they told the pilot, "Come on, let's get these three elk on the plane."

"Wait a minute! I can't get two guys, three elk, and all the equipment on the plane. We'll never make it," the pilot exclaimed.

"That's funny, you know last year...."

"All right, all right. If one bush pilot can make it, I guess I can." He loaded one elk and the gear on the left pontoon and the other two elk on the right. He pushed the little plane off the dock, revved up the motor, and shot down the lake. At the very end of the lake, the plane nosed into the air. It was just about clear before one pontoon caught a treetop and the plane flipped over and crashed on the side of a hill. After a time, one of the hunters woke up and said, "Where are we?"

His hunting buddy groaned, "We're about thirty feet further than last year—that's where we are."

Ladies and gentlemen, I want you to know that I'm not always right, but I'm never wrong!

A barnstorming pilot was touring Scotland selling rides in his open cockpit biplane. One day, he got into an argument with a stubborn Scot who insisted that he be allowed to bring his wife along at no extra cost. Finally, the pilot said, "Okay, I'll take you both up for the price of one, provided that you don't utter one sound."

"Okay."

The pilot and the couple climbed aboard. In the air, the pilot executed some death-defying stunts, but the Scotsman and his wife remained totally silent. After pulling every stunt from his bag of tricks, the pilot gave up and landed the plane.

"I don't believe it," the pilot called back as he taxied to a halt. "You're a very brave man."

"Thank yee," the Scot replied. "But I canna deny, there was one time when you almost had me."

"When was that?" the pilot asked.

"When my wife fell out, that's when!"

☙☙☙

LAUGHING AT LIFE • 197

When Tony Gordon was president of the life underwriters' association in the U.K., he was given a limousine and a chauffeur to drive him around. One day, according to Tony's wife, he was just outside of Bristol returning home from a trip. The car had stopped for a red light, and there was a knock on the window. Tony turned and saw a tramp standing there. He pushed the button and the window rolled down. Tony said to the bum, "What is it? What do you want?"

The bum looked at Tony and said, "Sir, please may I have five pounds for some food?"

Tony is a generous man, and he reached for his wallet. Then he reconsidered, "No. I'm not going to give you the five pounds. If I do, you will spend it on whisky."

"Sir," replied the bum, "You don't understand. I don't drink. I don't smoke, and I don't run around with wild women."

Tony jerked open the door and pulled the tramp inside, slammed the door shut, and instructed his chauffeur, "Quick, take me home."

The amazed bum asked, "What are you doing?"

"Nothing," Tony exclaimed, "I'm just going to take you home to show my wife what happens to someone who doesn't drink or smoke or chase wild women."

🐾🐾🐾

Once upon a time...! A young salesman was making preparations to attend a company conference. His wife asked him, "Are there going to be any women there?"

"Anybody in the field who qualified and some head office personnel will be there," he replied. As a matter of fact, there is going to be a costume party and dance on Friday night."

She looked at him slyly and said, "Why have you been so nice to me lately?"

"Well, I was hoping you could make a costume for me to wear to the party."

"What would you like to go as?", she queried.

"I'd like to be a brown tomcat, if you don't mind," he stated.

She chuckled, "Well you've passed that stage, but if you want to fool some people, its all right with me."

While she was sewing on this old brown tomcat costume, she got an idea that it might be fun to make herself a costume as well. On Friday, she could drive over to the party and check on her man. Now, she figured that the most normal thing for an old brown tomcat to pick out would be a little white kitten. Sure enough, on Friday, she showed up at the party in her little white kitten costume, and, as expected, the old tomcat found her right away. They danced and danced and danced, but never said a word, until suddenly the tomcat said, "I've never had such a good time at one of our conventions. Let me make a suggestion, if it doesn't seem to bold." He whispered, "Why don't we continue this party up in my hotel room?"

Disguising her voice and looking down slyly at the floor, she whispered hoarsely, "Okay, on condition that the lights be kept really, really low."

He readily agreed, and up to his room they went. (From here on let your imagination take over.)

Next day, she was waiting for her husband on the front porch when he got home from the convention. "Hi, honey. How did the convention go?", she inquired.

"Oh, so-so. There wasn't much to it," he answered.

"Well," she chuckled, "What I would really like to know about is the costume party on Friday night. How did it go?"

He snapped his fingers and said, "You know I meant to call you about that. I got sick and couldn't go to the dance, so I loaned my costume to another fellow, and he had one hell of a good time."

Yesterday is a memory.
Tomorrow is a dream.
Today is a real bitch.

Might doesn't always make right! Consider the following radio conversation recently released by a department of the U.S. Navy:

First voice: "Please divert your course fifteen degrees north to avoid collision."

Second voice: "Recommend you divert *your* course fifteen degrees south to avoid collision."

First voice: "This is the Captain of a U.S. naval ship. I say again, divert your course."

Second voice: "No, I say again, you divert *your* course."

First voice: This is the aircraft carrier *Enterprise*. We are on a large
warship of the U.S. Navy. Divert your course now!"
Second voice: "We are in the lighthouse. Your call!"

❦❦❦

Nido Qubein has some advice for salespeople: "Salespeople, when you
go on a call today, do not stick your foot in the door. Stick your head
in the door, so when they close it you can keep on talking."

Lily Tomlin said it so well:
"The trouble with the rat race is that,
even when you win, you are still a rat."

Three engineers and three mathematicians were traveling by train to a
conference. At the station, the three mathematicians each bought a ticket,
while they noticed that the three engineers bought only one ticket. One
curious mathematician asked, "How are three people going to travel on
only one ticket?" One of the engineers answered, "Watch and see."

They all boarded the train. The three mathematicians took their seats.
The three engineers crammed into a restroom and closed the door.
Shortly after the train departed, the conductor came around collecting
tickets. He knocked on the restroom door and said, "Ticket, please."

The door opened a crack, and one arm extended with the ticket. The
conductor took it and moved on, ticket in hand.

The mathematicians saw this, and they agreed that it was a clever
ploy. After the conference, they decided to copy the engineers and
save some money. They bought a single ticket for the return trip.
However, they were astonished to note that the engineers boarded the
train without purchasing even one ticket. "How are you going to travel
without even one ticket?", a perplexed mathematician asked.

"Watch and see," came the reply.

When the train started, the three mathematicians crammed into one
restroom. The engineers crowded into one nearby. Moments later, one of
the engineers left his restroom and walked over to the one in which the
mathematicians were hiding, knocked on the door and said, "Ticket,
please."

❦❦❦

What is the difference between mechanical engineers and civil engineers? Mechanical engineers built weapons. Civil engineers build targets.

❦❦❦

An engineering student was walking across campus when another engineer rode up on a shiny new motorcycle. "Where did you get such a great bike?", the student asked.

"Well, I was walking along yesterday, minding my own business when a beautiful woman rode up. She threw the bike on the ground and took off all of her clothes. Then she said, 'Take what you want.'"

"Good choice," said the first student. "The clothes probably wouldn't have fit."

It seems strange that they call money "dough."
After all, dough sticks to your fingers.

My friend Greg Wing made this contribution. (Greg sent some others as well, but they got edited out.)

Lying in a hospital bed, the dying old engineer began to flail about and make motions as if he would like to speak. The priest, who had been keeping watch at the bedside, leaned over and asked, "Do you have something to say?"

The old engineer nodded affirmatively, and the priest handed him a note pad and a pen. "I know you can't speak, but use this to write a note, and I'll make sure your wife gets it."

Gathering his last bit of strength, the old man took the pad and pen, scrawled his message, and stuffed it into the priest's hand. Moments later, he died.

After administering the last rites, the priest left to break the sad news to the dead man's wife. The priest consoled her for some time, then handed her the note. "Just before your husband passed on, he wrote a message to you."

The dead man's bereft wife took the note, carefully opened it, and read aloud: "Get your freakin' foot off my oxygen hose!"

❦❦❦

Knights of yore!

In the romantic days of knights and nobles, the kings knew the value of humor. A court jester was common in every court. His job was to entertain the knights and nobles and other guests of the king. As grist for the humor mill, no subject was forbidden, except, of course, ridicule of the king.

One day, the clever court jester went a little too far in doing an imitation of the king. The king was furious, and he ordered the court jester banished from his presence and put to death. "Off with his head," the king roared, as the jester was hauled away.

The knights and nobles of the court pleaded with the king for clemency. They begged him to reconsider. "After all, the jester had served the court long and well."

The king, however, had given an order that could not be rescinded. Nevertheless, hearing the pleas on behalf of the court jester, the king called the jester back and explained the situation. "I have ordered that you be put to death. I cannot change that order, but I can give you a choice of how you shall die."

The court jester, applying his quick wit, replied, "My lord, if it's all the same to you, I should like to die from a terminal case of old age."

❦❦❦

When I was a teenager, I really enjoyed the stories heard in the barbershop. Of course, men went to barbershops, and the women went to beauty parlors. The men told stories, and, as I hear it, the women gossiped. Today, many of us, both men and women, go to a hairstylist. There are still stories, but perhaps not so many, and not so ribald. Gossiping? Well, I don't know. Stefan Varnel has been my hairstylist for the past twenty-five years. We have shared a few stories. Stefan related the following one to me:

Two gentlemen saw each other quite frequently when they were walking their dogs in the park. They always nodded to one another. One day, they stopped and introduced themselves. They discovered they had many mutual interests. One of them suggested they continue their discussion over a beer. The other agreed, but wondered as they walked to a nearby pub, "What about our dogs? They'll not be allowed in."

The first chap with the German Shepherd said, "No problem, just follow my lead."

When he opened the door, the bartender advised him, "Sorry no dogs allowed in the bar."

"But this is a Seeing Eye dog," the owner of the German Shepherd replied.

"Oh, sorry, no problem then," the bartender commented.

Just then, the second dog owner approached with his dog.

"No dogs allowed in the bar, sorry sir," the barman repeated.

"Not even a Seeing Eye dog?", the second guy asked.

The amused barman chuckled: "A Seeing Eye dog? ... A Chihuahua?"

"What? Do you mean they sold me a Chihuahua?", queried the stunned would-be patron.

❦❦❦

Stefan enjoyed the story of an army corporal and a private getting simultaneous grooming. As he finished, the barber asked the corporal if he would like some refreshing cologne. "Gosh no," replied the corporal, "My wife would think I had visited a whore house."

The private chuckled, "I'll take some. My wife doesn't have any idea what a whore house smells like."

❦❦❦

Hey, guess what? Barbershops and hairstylist salons are a lot alike. However, the stylist charges one hell of a lot more than the barber did!

❦❦❦

An ad in a newspaper: "Lost dog. Walks on three legs. Missing right ear. Missing left eye. Recently castrated. Answers to the name 'Lucky'."

❦❦❦

There are hundreds of recipes for rabbit stew. They all start out the same way: "First get a rabbit."

❦❦❦

There is an old Jewish joke that states, "I'm an optimist. I believe that today will be better than tomorrow."

Getting a parking ticket is not as easy as you think. First, you've got to find a parking space.

I have always wanted a spicier voice mail message for our telephone answering. My niece Christine sent some suggestions:

- My wife and I can't come to the phone right now, but if you leave your name and number, we'll get back to you as soon as we are finished!
- Hi. A is for academics. B is for beer. One of those is the reason we're not here. So leave a message!
- Hello! If you leave a message, I'll call you soon. If you leave a sexy message, I'll call you sooner!
- Hi! Now you say something!
- Hello. I'm probably home. I'm just avoiding someone I don't like. Leave a message, and if I don't call you right back, it's you!
- Hello. You have reached Jim and Tonya. We can't pick up the phone right now, because we are doing something we really enjoy. Tonya likes doing it up and down. I like doing it right to left, real slowly. So leave a message and when we are done brushing our teeth, we'll call you back!

Kids' Stuff

Have you ever watched children at play? A lot goes on in those young minds! When I studied child psychology at university, one of my professors put it succinctly. She said, "There is nothing as complex as child's play." She defined a child psychologist as a person who tries to find out if children have more fun in infancy than adults do in adultery.

Children laugh easily and often. We should not overlook the fact that kids cry quite often as well. In fact, they go through the entire gamut of emotions on a regular basis. They can love and hate all in the same breath. They experience fight or flight reactions. Their wonderful imaginations permit them to envision all kinds of scary scenes. Ghosts in the closet, alligators in the bath tub, snakes under the bed, boogey men in the attic, and a variety of more recent creations, all provide material for the apparent need to experience the feeling of fear. No child, in my experience, goes laughing through the day strictly on happy mode. Perhaps the real secret of good healthy responses to life's changing events is the ability to release emotions. Children can and do let it all out. They are not afraid of telling the truth as they see it, even if someone's feelings get bruised a bit. In the directness of their answers, there is frequently humor.

If you lose the child within,
you lose the child without!

Art Linkletter had a TV program, you may remember, called "Kids Say the Darndest Things—People are Funny." Some of the things they said on his program probably had some parents laughing, and others crying, for many months. In keeping with my theme, "Humor is everywhere," I looked to my grandchildren and to other grandparents for inspiration.

Grandparents love to talk about their grandchildren, and why not? They are entertaining and energetic. Also, we can send them home when we get too tired.

One couple (grandparents) has a sign on the back of their camper that reads, "Let me tell you about our grandchildren." Another sign on the back of a car says, "Happiness is having grandchildren."

My wife likes the saying, "If I had known that grandchildren could be so much fun, I would have had them first."

The following are some of the incidents that I found to be funny.

☙☙☙

Recently, we invited our son, our daughter-in-law, and their three children to our condominium at Panorama, near Radium Hot Springs, British Columbia. The kids had never skied before, but they were excited about it. On the day of their arrival, we went up to the snow-covered hill between our condo and the ski slopes. Many children had been using it as a slide, which resulted in several well-worn paths. In order to slide down, it was necessary, first, to climb up. The boys, ages seven and eight, had no trouble clambering to the pinnacle. My son Darryl helped his soon-to-be five-year-old daughter.

After several slides, the boys tired of the game and wanted to explore the area. They left to ride the people-mover with their father. My granddaughter Spencer decided that she was having too much fun to leave with them. Of course, I stayed with her. As she started to climb, I moved up behind her, but I never helped her. She sensed my presence, looked back, and informed me in no uncertain terms, "I don't need any help."

"Okay, I won't help then."

She was able to proceed about three steps up before sliding back two. Finally, she lunged ahead about one and a half body lengths before sliding all the way back to where I was standing at the bottom. She looked at me in exasperation, as though I should be able to read her mind, and stated emphatically, "Well, you could help a little bit."

Eventually we both tired of the strenuous exercise, and I convinced her that we should go back to the condo to start the fireplace. Spencer agreed that would be fun. She looked around and asked, "But, where do we go?"

I told her, "You have to show me."

Without a moment's hesitation, she shouted, "Help, Help."

I calmed her with the suggestion that we could look at all the condos. Frankly, to a child who cannot read the numbers above the door, all these condos look alike. From our vantage, we could see that there was a large area to cover. She looked the situation over for a moment and then shouted, "Help, Help."

After we built the fire, I sat down at the table to read. Spencer brought her glass of Pepsi to me for safekeeping, while she went off on some errand. She cautioned me, "Don't drink any Grandpa, I already had a sip, and my germs are in there."

❦❦❦

Later, Darryl and I took the boys to the hot pool. To get down from the pool, we rode the people-mover, a sky tram from the ski slope to the housing complex. The boys were bundled up warmly. Austin, our seven-year-old, had a ski mask covering his face. As we reached the bottom, the young lady helping to unload us said, "Well, what have we got here, a masked man?"

Austin replied, "Yep, that's me."

I told her, "Watch out for him, he's the masked ladies' man."

"Oh," she queried, "so you like to chase the ladies, do you?"

"Yep," says Austin.

"Well, why do you like to chase the ladies?", she queried.

"I do it for the money," Austin quipped.

❦❦❦

We put the three kids in ski school, and for three days they labored on the bunny runs. On the third day, there was an incident that was not funny. Darryl and I were standing beside the boys as they waited in line for the rope tow. The boys had progressed to the next level at the top of the bunny run. We decided to go up to ski with them and watch them show their new skills. While waiting in line, two teenage snowboarders flashed through a narrow opening—airborne, no less. Both of them landed just inches in front of my skis with a loud "Whomp" and raced headlong into people merging from another slope.

I was surprised and shocked by this daring do. I shouted, "Smarten up, you young idiots."

One of them answered me, "You shouldn't be standing there."

"Idiots! You should not be racing down the bunny slope."

Later that evening, we took the family to a restaurant for dinner. While waiting for our orders, our youngest grandson Austin came to my end of the table and whispered, "Have you told Mom what happened today?"

I answered, "No. Why don't you tell her."

"Because it's your story," he replied.

When he went back to his place, he whispered to his mother, "When grandpa tells you about what happened today, pretend you haven't heard it already."

❧❧❧

Just outside the windows of the restaurant, there were several very artfully sculpted ice displays. We sat and admired them. I asked the kids, "What do they do with those sculptures when they melt?"

Our eldest grandson Logan answered, "They add water and freeze them up again."

Obviously, he doubts that it will ever be warm up there on the mountain. Number two grandson answered, "They make ice cubes out of them."

Our granddaughter stated emphatically, as is her style, "No-o, when they melt they make water out of them."

She likes to claim that girls are smarter than boys.

❧❧❧

We never had a daughter; just two boys. Now with a granddaughter we are enjoying a new experience. Little girls really are "Little Women." I agree with the words in the song, "They grow up in the most delightful way." She's only five years old, but already I feel that protectiveness common to most fathers. Recent statistics made me aware that peer pressure on young people is greater than ever to start having sex at ever-younger ages. In North America, 1.2 million teenage girls get pregnant every year. "No wonder," one person observed, "By the time the average teenager is sixteen, she or he has seen 72,500 TV scenes of implied sexual intercourse between unmarried people. There is no question that there is as much responsibility on boys as there is on girls when it comes to the question of sex."

One father had some advice for his daughter to which many of us can relate. If any of her boyfriends start to pressure her, this is what he advised her to say:

"So, you think it is okay for us to sleep together?"

And if he's pressuring her, he'll go, "Yep, I sure do. Uh-huh, uh-huh."

Now, daughter, you reply, "And you think you're a man, right?"

He'll reply, "Yep, I'm a man. I *am* a man!"

"And you're willing to stand up for the things you believe in?"

"Yep, I sure am."

"Well then, you talk to my father about it, and whatever he says is okay with me."

❦❦❦

Also, most fathers of daughters can relate to this father's reaction. When his teenage daughters were going out for the evening he heard his wife tell them, "Have fun!"

"No!" he shouted from upstairs. "Be good!"

People ask me
if I know a good definition of life. I tell them:
"Sure. Life is an incurable
sexually transmitted disease."

On Christmas day, in the year 2000, our four-year-old granddaughter slipped on the ice and cut her forehead. Her dad and I took her to the hospital, where, after three hours, she received six stitches.

Spencer was a little trouper and followed every instruction from the doctor. When the doctor completed her task, Darryl thanked her and asked Spencer if she could thank the doctor.

She replied, "Well, I could." But she never did.

The nurse made a fuss over Spencer, telling her what a brave little girl she had been. Spencer warmed up to her right away and informed her, "Girls are smarter than boys, you know."

The nurse turned to me and asked, "What does Grandpa say about that?"

"Well, whatever she says is okay, I guess. After all, she does have two older brothers."

❧❧❧

Age four seems to be the age when kids say the darndest things. Our eldest grandson, at age four, came up with a shocker one day. Grandma called to ask if the family would like to come over for dinner. Stacy turned to Logan and asked, "Do you want to go to Grandma's for dinner?"

"What is she having?", he questioned.

"Chicken."

"What kind of chicken?"

"Well, just chicken."

"Not that 'f—ken' cheese chicken, I hope," came the shocker.

Oops! Mother sat him down and informed him, "Young man, in this family, we do not use that kind of language."

He has not said that word since—at least, not when his mother can hear it. Where did a four-year-old pick up that word? He did not learn it from Grandpa. No he did not!

❧❧❧

Age four seems to be a magical time for kids. Anything is possible—everything is attainable. One day, when Austin was three and Logan was four, Darryl took them shopping with him. He was on a frugal shopping trip. That is where we men try to prove to the distaff side of the family that we can shop just as smartly as they do. Darryl checks prices in his palm pilot. That's his advantage.

Anyway, Logan spotted some luscious plums and just had to have one. Darryl looked them over and stated bluntly: "They are too expensive. We can't afford them." They continued shopping, but Logan was not mollified. In fact, a little later he asked, "Daddy, can't we afford *just one*?" Darryl relented, of course.

☙☙☙

About age four, Logan came shopping with me. After a while, we walked past a Macdonald's restaurant—well, almost past. Logan grabbed my hand and said, "Pappa, I'm hungry." (So what's new kid?)
So I said to him, "Do you have any money?'
"No," he stated.
"Well what are you going to eat then?", I asked.
Logan replied, "Well, I don't eat money!"

☙☙☙

Before Logan turned four, he had trouble getting his shoes on the right feet. Stacy told him again for the umpteenth time, "Logan your shoes are on the wrong feet."
Logan grimaced at her and replied, "But Mom, they're the only feet I got."
That's logical, isn't it?

☙☙☙

When our number-two grandson was about four and a half years old, he decided that he would not eat certain things. That's no problem; lot's of little people go through periods of strange eating habits. However, it was the obstinate attitude that Austin affected that caused the trouble. A dialogue between the little rascal and his parents went something like this:

Austin: "I don't like pasta."
Mom: "Too bad. You better eat it. That's all your going to get."
Austin: "Can I save it for a snack later?"
Dad: "Eat it, or there's no dessert."
Later, still with no dessert, Austin complains, "That pasta will give me a stomach ache."

Aunt Kiffy (a nurse whose real name is Cathy) answered, "No, it won't, Austin."

Austin: "Then it will give me a headache."

Aunt Kiffy: "No, it won't, Austin."

Austin: "Then it will give me measles."

Aunt Kiffy: "No, Austin, pasta will not give you a headache, nor a stomach ache, nor measles, nor mumps, nor anything bad, but it might get you some dessert."

Austin: "Well then, fine."

Several days later, Austin came down with chicken pocks. Aunt Kiffy asked, "Well, what happened to you, Austin?"

Without a moments hesitation, Austin replied, "It must have been the pasta."

❧❧❧

When Austin started Kindergarten, he met a sweet young girl, and they became inseparable friends. One day when Stacy went to pick the kids up from school, she discovered Austin and Suzy holding hands. Austin introduced Suzy to his mom and informed her that soon they would get married.

Stacy asked Austin about his sister, Spencer. "Yesterday, you told me that you were going to marry Spencer."

"Yeah," replied Austin, "But you said I couldn't marry my sister."

"That's right, you can't."

"Well," stated Austin, "I'll have to marry Suzy, then."

❧❧❧

In kindergarten, Austin preferred to follow his own agenda, rather than the one provided by the teacher, which, as you know, meant that he was in trouble quite often. His teacher had a system of giving sad faces for bad behavior and happy faces for good behavior. After a few days, Austin's teacher showed him his chart, which went sad face, happy face, sad face, and so on. She asked, "What do you think of that, Austin?"

Undaunted by this confrontation with the evidence of his activities, he stated bluntly, openly, innocently, "Looks like I've got a pattern."

Choking back her need to laugh, his teacher replied, "Yes, but not necessarily the one you should have."

It worked. After that, he strove to get happy faces.

❧❧❧

When Spencer was two, she still did not talk plainly. We wondered if she was ever going to talk. Now we wonder if she will ever stop talking. However, until about the age of two, she would gesture and mumble something that both her brothers seemed to understand. I asked our eldest grandson, Logan, why Spencer didn't talk. He replied, "She can talk if she wants to."

"Well, why doesn't she try to talk?", I asked.

"She doesn't need to talk," Logan informed me.

I suggested to those present, "Let's make her talk if she wants something, okay?" Everyone agreed with me that we would make her ask for what she wanted. Before long, she wanted a glass of milk, but she wouldn't ask for it. She just mumbled and pointed. Spencer went first to her mother, and Stacy told her, "Ask for what you want."

She then went to Grandma, who gave her the same advice. She whined for a moment and then approached Grandpa. She took me by the hand, placed it on the refrigerator door, and tugged until I opened it. Then she pointed to the milk, and Grandpa gave in.

Those assembled gave Grandpa a bad time. "It was your idea to make her talk."

"Logan is right," I replied, "She doesn't need to talk."

❧❧❧

Spencer could talk well enough when she wanted her mother to understand her. One day, Stacy walked into Spencer's room to find clothing all over the floor. Immediately, Spencer started scolding her mother for strewing her clothing around. Obviously, she had learned that to attack first is the best defense.

❧❧❧

When Spencer was about three years old, she said to me, "Grandpa, get me a glass of milk."

I didn't like the tone of her demand, so, of course, I said, "What's the magic word?'

"NOW!" she shouted.

☙☙☙

My family says Grandpa is a soft touch, and they point to the bicycle incident as proof of the allegation. Out of the blue one day, Austin asked Grandma for a bicycle. Grandma told him, "Not yet, you are too young."

Austin is not easily deterred. He continued to badger Grandma for a bicycle until she told him, "We are not even going to discuss it."

Deflated, but not defeated, Austin approached Grandpa. I asked, "What did Grandma say?"

Austin admitted, "She said we are not going to discuss it."

"Okay, so that's it then. Right?"

"Well, but what do you say, Grandpa?"

"Uh, let me talk to your Grandma." (He got the bicycle.)

☙☙☙

Recently, Austin found a brightly colored bead, similar, I suspect, to those in the strand of beads that were used to purchase Manhattan Island. He was quite proud of it and refused to give it to his sister, who coveted it. Later, Darryl noticed that Spencer had the bead in her possession. He asked Austin, "Did you give your bead to Spencer?"

"Well," Austin answered, "she sort of earned it."

"Oh, how did she earn it?", Darryl queried.

"She took my fire safety course."

At school, Austin had been learning about fire safety in the home.

"So," questioned Darryl, "Spencer is the first graduate of your fire safety program, right?"

Austin leaned toward his parents conspiratorially and whispered, "She didn't actually graduate, but I just got tired of teaching her."

☙☙☙

Several years ago, when my brother visited an elderly gentleman in an old folk's home, he took his young son Robbie with him. They found the old boy in the sunroom sound asleep. In fact, the elderly gent was snoring quite loudly. The sound rather frightened Robbie. Grant asked, "What's wrong, Robbie, can't you do that?"

"No," whispered Robbie, "I never learned that yet."

Grant's second son, Kenny, has always been mechanically inclined. Whenever his father was busy doing something, young Ken would be right in there to *help* his dad. One day, after installing new carpet, Grant was tacking the baseboards back on. Kenny kept getting in the way, so Grant told him, "Kenny move your head."

Well, Kenny, with the innocence of a four-year-old, asked, "Where do you want me to put it?"

❧❧❧

Paul, a young lad who lives with his family in my brother's neighborhood, went to church every Sunday morning with his mother. Every Sunday, Paul's mother told him, "We are going to God's house so you must stay clean and behave."

Every Sunday, the priest stood up in the pulpit and gave a sermon. After two years, a baby sister was old enough to go with them, and the routine continued. One day, when Paul's mother was changing a new baby's diaper, the doorbell rang. Since she was up to her elbows in it, she instructed Paul to answer the door. When he opened it, there stood the priest. Paul shouted, "Mom, God's here!"

❧❧❧

Grant wrote to me about another situation. He speaks French fluently and has spent some time in Paris. He told me, Parisians believe they are protectors of the French language, and they are quick to correct anyone who would believe otherwise. Some of Grant's friends were posted to Paris for a year, and they lived near the Eiffel Tower. After the first term, they were reassigned for an additional three years. Their young son John had been immersed in French school for a year and a half and had become quite proficient in the French language. One day while riding on a bus, an elderly couple sat down next to John. In French, the elderly gent said, "Do you know that the Eiffel Tower twinkles every night?"

John answered in French, "Yes, it's been doing this since Christmas."

Of course, the elderly couple had no way of knowing that John lived near the tower. The elderly lady said to her husband, "I'll bet that he is bilingual."

That was the opening that John needed. He replied, "Oui, et je parle français mieux que toi." (The perfect putdown for a Parisian.)

(Well, Canada is a bilingual country—you translate it.)

❦❦❦

Rosemary Hooper contributed the following. She says, "Aren't kids great?"

The boss of a big company needed to speak to one of his employees about an urgent problem with one of the main computers. He dialed the employee's home number and was greeted by a child who whispered, "Hello."

Feeling put out at having to speak to a child, the boss asked, "Is your Daddy home?"

"Yes," whispered the small voice.

"May I speak to him?", the man asked.

To the surprise of the boss, the small voice answered, "No."

Wanting to speak to an adult, the boss asked, "Is your Mommy there?"

"Yes," came the answer.

"May I talk to her?"

Again the small voice whispered, "No."

Knowing that a small child would not be there alone, the boss decided to leave a message with the person who should be watching over the child. He asked, "Is anyone there besides you?"

"Yes," whispered the child, "a policeman."

Wondering what a cop would be doing at his employee's home, the boss asked, "May I speak to the policeman?"

"No, he's busy," whispered the child.

"Busy doing what?" Asked the boss.

"Talking to Mommy and Daddy and the fireman," she whispered in reply.

Growing concerned and even worried as he heard through the ear what sounded like a helicopter, the boss asked, "What's that noise?"

"A hello-copper," answered the whispered voice.

"What's going on there?" queried the alarmed boss.

In an awed whispering voice, the child stated, "The search team just landed the hello-copper!"

Alarmed, concerned, and more than a little frustrated, the boss asked, "What are they doing there?"

Still whispering, the young voice replied in a muffled giggle, "They're looking for me!"

I am an Indian

Recently, our friends Shri and Kunda Pratinidhi visited us in Calgary. Their visit reminded us of an earlier trip to our home, when our eldest son, Scott, was just five years old. This lovely couple originally came from India. Kunda usually wears a beautiful sari, but Shri (pronounced "Shree") wears only Canadian-style clothes. On the second day of their visit, Scott dressed in his cowboy outfit from head to toe: cowboy boots, western hat, gun belt with holsters and toy guns. He made lots of five-year-old noise.

"What are you doing?", queried Shri. "Are you playing cowboys and Indians?

"Yes," answered Scott, "and I'm looking for Indians."

"Well, I'm an Indian," says Shri.

Without hesitation Scott told him, "No you're not."

Shri insisted, "Oh yes, I am!"

Scott was emphatic, "No you're not!

Shri chuckled, "Why do you say I am not an Indian?"

Scott answered knowingly, "No feathers!"

ಆಆಆ

Many years ago, my friend Bill Clennan and I took our boys skating on an outside rink. My sons could already skate, but Bill's boy Jay had never been on skates before, and he was quite a bit younger than my two boys. When the skates were tied, Scott and Darryl took off with gleeful abandon. In fact, they abandoned Jay, who wanted to skate with them.

Jay strode forth with youthful exuberance, only to fall flat on the ice. He managed to stand up, take one more stride, and down he went again. We offered our assistance, but Jay obstinately refused it. If Scott and Darryl could do it, then Jay was determined that he could succeed on his own.

After several additional failing attempts, Jay crawled over to a makeshift bench and sat down, head in hands, elbows on knees. He was pouting, thoroughly discouraged and almost in tears. We offered to help him learn to skate, but no way.

Bill asked him, "Why don't you take my hand and skate with me?"

"No!"

I offered my hand: "Come, Jay, skate between your dad and me."

"No!"

"Well, why not, Jay?", his dad asked solicitously.

"I'm just going to sit here until I learn to skate," the reasoned reply came.

My house

When Bill Clennan found that his new career as a professional speaker kept him away from Calgary for months at a time, his solution was to take his wife and young son, Jay, with him. They stored some of their things at our home, and when they were in Calgary they stayed with us.

For Jay, this was home—his home. Naturally, as part of our expanded family, Jay got the same treatment as our sons. The same rules applied to all of them—no exceptions. Jay was about four years old, that magic age when kids say what they think and mean what they say. My title with Jay was Daddy-Lyle. That's what he called me!

Now, one day, Jay was bending one of my rules just a touch too far, so, of course, I gave him my Daddy-Lyle advice: "Jay, stop that right now!"

Well! Jay looked at me with all the defiance of a four-year-old, put his hands on his hips and shouted, "Daddy-Lyle, get out of my house!"

ଙଙଙ

Adults frequently ask teenagers what they plan to do, or what they want to be when they grow up. One teenager offered an explanation for this parental questioning: "They are still looking for good ideas for themselves."

ଙଙଙ

Three young boys were sitting on a curb reading magazines. An adult neighbor stopped to say hi to the lads. She noticed that Billy was reading *Popular Mechanics*.

"What are you going to be when you grow up, Billy?"

Without hesitation, he replied, "I'm going to be a race car driver."

She noticed that Ronald was reading a medical journal. "And what do you plan to be, Ronnie?", she inquired.

"I'm going to be a psychiatrist," stated the thoughtful youth.

"That's wonderful, both of you, and Johnny, what—whoa, what is this?", she challenged, as she grabbed the copy of *Playboy* magazine from young lad. "What do you think you will grow up to be looking at stuff like this, Johnny?"

"Well," answered the lad, "I don't know what you call it, but I can hardly wait to get started."

❡❡❡

For a Kindergarten project, the children were required to interview a working parent to find out what he or she does for a living on a daily basis. They were expected to report back to the class on the interview. One little girl approached her father. He was a life insurance salesman, and for forty-five minutes he explained what he did for people.

The next day in class she reported, "My daddy talks to people until they die."

❡❡❡

Here are some conundrums for children and the young at heart:

- *Q:* Why are fish so smart?
  A: They live in schools.
  (One of life's little mysteries revealed there.)

- *Q:* What's the difference between a jeweler and a jailer?
  A: One sells watches and the other watches cells.

- *Q:* Why do we call money 'bread'?
  A: Because everybody kneads it.

- *Q:* What did Batman say to Robin when he went to get in the car?
  A: Robin, get in the car.

- *Q:* Where does an 800-pound gorilla sleep?
  A: Anywhere it wants.

- *Q:* Why does an elephant paint it's toenails different colors?
  A: So he can hide in a Smarties box.
  (Ever seen an elephant in a Smarties box? Hides pretty good, right?)

- Q: Why did the whale cross the ocean?
  A: To get to the other tide.

Some people may think these silly things are not all that funny, but they will probably giggle in their sleep at night.

❧❧❧

One day, a little boy and his dad were behind a large lady when her pager started to beep. "Look out Dad," said the young lad, "I think she's going to back up."

❧❧❧

Try to find a word in the dictionary that rhymes with any of the following words: orange, purple, silver, month.

If you suppress a laugh, it goes back down and expands your hips.

- *Q:* Why are the middle ages also called the dark ages?
  A: Because there were so many knights.

- *Q:* What do you call a cow that can't give milk?
  A: An udder failure.

- *Q:* What's the difference between a hill and a pill?
  A: A hill is hard to get up, and a pill is hard to get down.

- *Q:* How many times can you subtract 2 from 21?
  A: Only once. After the first time, you would be
     subtracting 2 from 19, then 17, 15, and so on.

- *Q:* Who earns a living driving people away?
  A: A taxi driver!

- *Q:* How much did the pirate pay when he had his ears pierced?
  A: A buck an ear!

- *Q:* Why don't they grow bananas any longer?
  A: Bananas are long enough already!

- *Q:* How can you communicate with a fish?
  A: Drop him a line!

- *Q:* What has a bed but does not sleep?
     What has a mouth but does not speak?
  A: A river!

A little boy asked his grandfather, "How did you get up in that tree, Grandpa?"

"I sat on an acorn," he answered.

❦❦❦

When I was a young lad, one of my parents' dearest friends used to tell us funny stories. "Jack" was small in stature, only 5 foot 4, so we kids could relate to him readily. He and Aunt Florence used to visit us regularly. They had no children of their own, so we became their surrogate kids. One story Jack loved to tell was about a garter snake and a frog.

"One time when I was fishing on the bank of a small lake in northern Ontario, I heard a little squeak. Looking down, I saw a garter snake with a frog in its mouth. Quickly, I grabbed a small bottle of whisky that I had with me for medicinal purposes. I poured a couple of drops into the snake's mouth, and he let the frog go."

We were country boys; we giggled, but we did not believe him.

"Oh yes," he assured us, "Not only that, why it wasn't five minutes later the same snake returned with another frog in its mouth."

❦❦❦

We raised chickens on our farm. We had lots and lots of little hatchlings. They were fun to watch as they scurried around looking for food. Jack asked us, "Can you boys tell the difference between little girl chicks and little boy chicks?"

"No. Can you?"

"Well," answered Jack, "I didn't used to know, so I consulted a chicken expert. Do you know what he told me?"

"No," we answered skeptically, "how can you tell?"

"Its easy," Jack replied. "You get a pan of worms from the garden for the chicks and watch them eat. The little boy chicks will eat the little girl worms and the little girl chicks will eat the little boy worms."

"Oh yeah?", we challenged. "How can you tell which worms are little girl worms and which ones are little boy worms?"

Jack chuckled, "Well I asked the guy the same question. Do you know what he told me?"

"No, what?"

"He said, 'Heck man, I'm a chicken expert, not a worm expert. You will have to consult a worm expert.'"

❦❦❦

Father took his four-year-old son to see a litter of kittens. When they returned home, the young lad excitedly told his mom, "We saw two boy kittens and two girl kittens."

"How did you know?", his mother asked.

Daddy picked them up and looked underneath," he answered. "I think it's printed on the bottom."

❦❦❦

Some time ago, a little girl was riding in the car with her mother on a freeway. Traffic, as always, was bad. The little girl could barely peer over the dash. After being quiet for a while, she asked her mother, "Where are all the stupid bastards today?"

"Oh, I don't know," her mother chuckled. "I guess they are only out when your father drives."

❦❦❦

When you are out on a limb,
try using your head!

One day, a little boy and his father found a bag containing nearly one thousand dollars in it. The father said to his son: "Now, son, there is a question of ethics here. The question is, should we tell your mom about it?"

❦❦❦

Recently, after a business trip to Toronto, my son went down to the farm to visit his grandmother. He called and talked to his family every day, but, on one of his calls from the farm, the line was not too clear. When Darryl finished talking to his five-year-old daughter, he asked, "Have you got a kiss for me?"

"What?" she challenged.

"Do you have a kiss for me?"

"No! I don't have any kids. I'm not an adult. Duh!"

❦❦❦

Children are great imitators. They imitate their parents, and they imitate other young people, especially those they like.

When Allan was a teenager, he didn't like himself very much. He wanted to be like Billy Widdledon, and Billy didn't even like him. Anyway, Allan walked and talked like Billy. He even went to the same high school. And that was when Billy began to change. Billy began hanging around with Herbie Vandeman. He walked like Herbie, and he talked like Herbie. Allan was getting confused because he was walking and talking like Billy Widdledon, and Billy was walking and talking like Herbie Vandeman. Then Allan noticed that Herbie was walking and talking like Joey Haverlan, and Joey was walking and talking like Corky Sabinson.

"So," says Allan, "there I was walking and talking like Billy Widdledon's version of Herbie Vandeman's imitation of Joey Haverlan walking and talking like Corky Sabinson. And who do you think Corky was walking and talking like? Of all the people, Corky was walking like Dopey Wellington, that little pest who was walking and talking like me."

❦❦❦

Recently, a seven-year-old kid went to his teacher and asked, "How come I'm failing in your class, and my friend Johnny is getting a 'C'?"

"Because you copied on the test," his teacher answered.

"I did not copy. You don't like me. I'm going to bring my mom."

The teacher thought the kid was joking, but, next day, there comes his mom. "Why is my son failing in your class when his friend Johnny is getting a 'C'?"

The teacher gave the same answer, "Because he copied the test."

The mother defended her son, "Oh, he did not copy. You just don't like him. And furthermore, you can't prove he copied."

The teacher went to his desk, pulled out the tests and proceeded to explain to the mother. "Here is Johnny's test, and this is your son's test.

Question #1, well done Johnny. Your son's—correct.
Question #2, Johnny—perfect. Your son's—I have no objection.
Question #3, Johnny—perfect. Your son's—neatly done.
Question #4, Johnny wrote, 'I don't know.' Your son wrote, 'Me either.'

☙☙☙

One day, when one of our friends was out shopping with his four year-old granddaughter, she shocked him suddenly with a statement made loud enough for everyone in the store to hear: "Grandpa, boys fart. Girls only toot!"

☙☙☙

This same grandpa used to teach a Sunday school class for six- and seven-year-olds. After each session, he would have the children draw pictures of what they had just learned. On one occasion, he taught them the story of Adam and Eve in the Garden of Eden. As before, he instructed the young students to draw a picture about the story. One little boy drew trees, including an apple tree, flowers and shrubs, and so on. It was quite well done. However, this lad drew an automobile in the picture. So our friend told the boy, "There was no car in the Garden of Eden. Cars were not even invented until many years after all of the people had left the Garden of Eden."

"Oh no, there had to be a car," the youth stated confidently. "You said God *drove* Adam and Eve from the Garden of Eden."

❦❦❦

Reverend Mr. Peter Maunsell, pd, told me an interesting story:

After church, one day, mother asked her young son what he had learned in Sunday school. He replied excitedly, "We learned about Moses and his people escaping from the Egyptian Pharaoh."

"And how did they do that?", his mother prompted.

Her son explained, "They ran down to the Red Sea, and they were stuck because they couldn't get across. The Pharaoh and his army were right behind them."

"So what did they do?", his mother queried.

"They built a pontoon bridge and pushed it across the lake. Then they walked over the bridge to the other side. The Pharaoh's army was right behind them. They waited until the army was in the middle of the bridge, then they took a rocket and blew up the bridge and the army drowned."

"Oh my," his mother commented. "Is that the story your teacher told you?"

After a moment's hesitation, her young son answered, "No, but you would never believe the story she told us."

❦❦❦

One morning a mother went into the bathroom while her young son was in the bathtub. She noticed something that made her curious. Her son was very quietly concentrating intently on something. He was lying in water up to his neck. She asked him, "What are you doing, Tommy?"

He replied, "Experimenting."

That didn't surprise her too much since she had been showing the children how to do certain experiments. For example, they had filled four beakers with water. One glass contained cold salt water. Another was prepared with hot salt water. The other two were plain water, one hot and one cold. To each of these, they added a few drops of different-colored food coloring. Then they carefully poured a little from each beaker into another glass. They were able to determine which was heaviest and which one was lightest. The heaviest concoction went to the bottom and the lightest to the top. That was only one of the experiments they had done together. Now her son was conducting his own experiment—obviously not one she had taught him. He was lying there passing wind and watching the bubbles come up through the water. She chuckled and asked, "Oh, tell me about your experiment." So he told her, "I'm trying to find out if farts smell better after they pass through water." Smart kid!

❦❦❦

Another grandpa went out to watch his grandson play sandlot ball. It seems to be a duty for grandparents to watch the little tykes demonstrate their skills in one sport or another. As he walked down the third base line, he asked the fielder at third base, "What's the score?"

The little tyke answered, "There's no one out, the bases are loaded, and it's 43 to 0."

He chuckled and asked, "You're getting beat, aren't you?"

"Nope," replied the lad, "Not yet, we're not. Our side ain't been to bat, and it ain't over 'til we win!"

❦❦❦

One father was going through customs accompanied by his young son. The customs officer asked the usual questions.

"Do you have anything to declare?"

"No."

"Do you have any tobacco?"

"No."

"Any alcohol?"

"No."

"Any camera film, etc.?"

"No, no."

At this point, the young lad looked at his dad and said, "But he's getting warmer; right Dad?"

Oops!

❦❦❦

Another grandfather told his daughter that he was going to take his young grandson to the zoo. She thought that was a great idea. (It got both of them out from under her feet, so to speak.)

Later, when they returned home, she asked, "Well, Donny, did you enjoy the zoo?"

"Yeah, it was exciting," the lad replied. "One of the animals paid $48.50 across the board."

What sound do porcupines make when they kiss?
"Ouch!"

Our friends Trevor and Lorraine Lawrence sent us the following stories:

Mother was preparing pancakes for her sons, Kevin (age five) and Ryan (age three). The boys were arguing over who would get the first pancake. Their mother saw the opportunity for a moral lesson. She said, "If Jesus were here, he would say 'Let my brother have the first pancake. I can wait.'"

Kevin turned to his younger brother and said, "Ryan, you be Jesus."

❧❧❧

After the church service, a five-year-old boy told the pastor, "When I grow up, I'm going to give you some money."

"Why, thank you, but why?", the pastor asked.

"Because my daddy says you're one of the poorest preachers we have ever had."

❧❧❧

When mother invited some people for dinner, she thought to show off her six-year-old daughter's ability. She turned to her daughter and asked, "Would you like to say the blessing?"

The little girl answered, "I don't know what to say."

"Just say what you hear mommy say."

"Okay." The little girl bowed her head and said, "Lord, why on earth did I invite all these people to dinner?"

❧❧❧

When one mother was teaching her three-year-old daughter the Lord's prayer, the little girl repeated it faithfully for several evenings in a row. Then one evening she felt that the child was ready to go solo. She listened with pride as her daughter carefully enunciated the words right up to the end: "And lead us not into temptation, but deliver us from e-mail."

❦❦❦

Her son was looking at the family Bible with fascination. As he carefully turned the pages, a leaf suddenly fell out. He picked it up and looked at it studiously. It was an old leaf that had been pressed between the pages.

"Mommy, look what I found," the boy called out.

"What have you got, son?" his mother asked.

Reverently her son answered, "I think it is Adam's suit."

❦❦❦

When mother and her young son returned from the grocery store, they began putting the groceries away. She noticed that her son had opened a box of animal crackers and was spreading them all over the counter.

"What are you doing?", she asked.

"The box says not to eat them if the seal is broken," her son explained. "I'm looking for the seal."

❦❦❦

One morning, a father overheard his two young sons talking. David, the eldest, instructed his younger brother: "Joel, this morning we will talk like adults. When we get to the breakfast table and Mom asks what I want for breakfast, I'm going to use a sentence with the word 'hell' in it. When Mom asks what you want, you use a sentence with the word 'damn' in it. That way we will sound like adults."

Sure enough, mother asked, "David, what can I get you for breakfast?"

David answered, "Hell, Mom, I think I'll take some Cheerios."

His mother's reaction was not what he expected. She knocked him out of his chair, grabbed him, put him over her knee, and spanked him soundly. "Now, young man, get to your room, and don't come out until I come for you."

She walked over to her younger son and asked, "Now, young man, what can I get you for breakfast?"

As adult as possible, Joel answered, "Well, it damned sure won't be Cheerios."

ϑϑϑ

This kid in high school went up to a girl who really couldn't stand him. He said right out, "If you can guess what I have between my hands I'll take you to the dance Saturday night."

In an aloof manner, she answered, "An elephant!"

Excitedly, the youth replied, "That's close enough. What time do I pick you up?"

ϑϑϑ

When Professor Anthony Clare interviewed mentalist Uri Geller on his radio show, he asked Geller. "You were an only child, right? Do you know why?" Geller replied, "Yes, because my parents didn't have any other children.

ϑϑϑ

Here is a slightly modernized version of a classic Christmas poem. We hope you will like it:

'Twas the Night before Christmas

'Twas the night before Xmas when all through the house,
Not a creature was stirring, not even a computer mouse.

The stockings were hung by the chimney with care,
In the hopes that St Nicholas soon would be there.

The children were nestled all snug in their beds,
While visions of CD-ROMs, Play Stations,
      and personal computers danced in their heads.

Mamma in her kerchief and I in my cap,
Had just settled in for a long winter's nap.

When out in the yard there arose such a clatter,
I sprang from my bed to see what was the matter.

Away to the window I flew like a flash,
I tore open the shutter, and threw up the sash.

The moon on the breast of the new fallen snow,
Gave a luster of midday to objects below.

When what to my wondering eyes should appear,
But a miniature sleigh, and eight tiny reindeer.

Excuse me! That's my spot and you're in it,
And you don't even have a parking permit.
Could you just take it somewhere else?

As I turned from the ledge in a bit of a huff,
They flew past the edge, up to the roof.

Up to the rooftop the coursers they flew,
With a sleigh full of toys and Santa Claus too.

Then in a twinkling I heard them stop,
And start prancing and pawing on our new rooftop.

Ahoy there! You and your team up on the roof,
Don't you know it can be damaged by one tiny hoof?

The condo association just spent $35,000 (American),
    to do a restore.
Can't you park in the driveway, and come in through
    the door?

As I drew in my head and was turning around,
Down the chimney he came with a bound.

He was dressed all in fur from his head to his foot,
And his clothes were all tarnished with ashes and soot.

A bundle of toys he had flung on his back,
And he looked like a peddler just opening his pack.

His eyes—how they twinkled! His dimples—how merry,
His cheeks were like roses, his nose like a cherry.

His droll little mouth was drawn up like a bow,
And the beard on his chin was as white as the snow.

The stump of a pipe he held tight in his teeth,
And the smoke encircled his head like a wreath.

I say, I know you're a saint, and by that I abide,
But if you must smoke, could you take it outside?

He had a broad face and a round little belly,
That shook when he laughed, like a bowlful of jelly.

He was chubby and plump, a right jolly old elf,
And I laughed when I saw him in spite of myself.

A wink of his eye and a twist of his head,
Soon gave me to know I had nothing to dread.

He spoke not a word, but went straight to his work,
And filled all the stockings, I felt like a jerk.

No longer does Santa make a list and check it twice,
He consults his Palm Pilot to find any vice.

He filled the kids stockings with candy and toys,
Sugar plums for the girls and tiny racecars for the boys.

Then with a chuckle he lay a finger by his nose,
And giving a nod, up the chimney he rose.

He sprang to his sleigh, to his team gave a whistle,
And away they flew like the down of a thistle.

On Monitor, on Hacker, on Senate, and on Triple E,
He shouted their names as he chuckled with glee.

But I heard him exclaim as he flew out of sight,
Merry Christmas to all and to all a good night!

Even you, Lyle!"

❦❦❦

He who laughs last, thinks slowest!

Here's a thought! Send everyone you know a
card next year that says it all.
Happy Everything; New Years day, Birthday,
Valentines day, Easter, St. Patrick's day, Mothers
day, Firecracker day, Fathers day, Daffidol day,
Canada day, Hanuka, Halloween, Thanksgiving,
and Merry Christmas.

If I had my child to raise again.
I'd finger paint more,
    And point my finger less.
I'd do less correcting,
    And more connecting.
I'd take my eyes off my watch,
    And watch with my eyes.
I'd care to know less,
    And know to care more.
I'd take more hikes,
    And fly more kites.
I'd stop playing seriously,
    And seriously play.
I'd run through more fields,
    And gaze at more stars.
I'd do more hugging,
    And less tugging.
I' d be firm less often,
    And affirm much more.
I'd build self esteem first,
    And the house later.
I'd teach less about the love of power,
    And more about the power of love.

Author Unknown

Index

238 • LAUGHING AT LIFE

About the Author

"Laughing at life" is Lyle Manery's motto. He looks for humor in every situation in which he finds himself.

> If you can't laugh at yourself, and at the *faux pas* you make, you are too serious. Lighten up and take time to smell the daisies.

For over fifty years, Lyle has been accumulating humorous incidents and anecdotes. On the more serious side, Lyle has written and published several other books, including:

No Salesman Will Call
Network Marketing Success for Everyone
Legends, Lies and Myths of Financial Planning
Vital Knowledge for Your Retirement Planning

Dawg (published on our website)

For more information about these books, see our website at **www.lyaltapub.com** or call toll-free to order: **1-888-322-2558**

No Salesman Will Call

$18.95; 278 pp., softcover

In this book, the author critiqued the written and published material of over fifty other authors. The common theme among these writers was what's wrong with your life insurance. They wrote about the evils of the products available, the companies that offered them, and the salespeople who sold them. Research determined that these writers had no credentials to criticize. Nevertheless, they wrote authoritatively on a subject on which they had very little knowledge. None of them had any practical experience in the field. And yet, to this author's chagrin, and to the displeasure of other knowledgeable people in the industry, they were frequently quoted as authorities.

This book takes the common arguments and shows where the writers erred. It proves, with facts and figures, that the information provided was erroneous, misleading, and terribly biased. *No Salesman Will Call* is filled with facts based on the author's forty-plus years of experience.

Network Marketing Success for Everyone

$19.95; 192 pp. softcover

Why do so many people join one or more multi-level marketing or consumer direct organizations, with little or no success? Why do the recruits of those who do achieve some success fail to live up to their potentials?

This book shows you how to do the business successfully. If you are going to be in the business, why not do it right? The original version, *Eclectic Mushrooms for the Wealthy Network Marketer*, was written as a training manual for the author's own down-line.

Network Marketing Success for Everyone was expanded to provide sales training material that can be applied by anyone in any sales program. The basic principles are directed at network marketing, but they are beneficial for anyone in sales.